The Power of
**Social
Intelligence**

The Power of
Social
Intelligence

Tony Buzan

Thorsons

Thorsons
An Imprint of HarperCollins*Publishers*
77–85 Fulham Palace Road
Hammersmith, London W6 8JB

The Thorsons website address is: www.thorsons.com

and *Thorsons* are registered trademarks of HarperCollins*Publishers* Ltd

First published 2002

10 9 8 7 6

Plate section illustrations by Alan Burton

A catalogue record for this book
is available from the British Library

ISBN 0 7225 4048 5

Printed and bound in Great Britain by
Martins the Printers Ltd, Berwick upon Tweed

dedication

This book is dedicated to the celebration of the extraordinary Social Intelligence of my friend and Personal Assistant, Lesley Bias, and to the 20th anniversary of our working together. During that time Lesley has dealt personally with hundreds of thousands of people from all walks of life and from approximately 100 different countries around the world. She is universally admired and held in great affection.

Lesley, this one's for you!

contents

list of Mind Maps®

Summary Mind Map® of Chapter 2 – Who Am I? – how you project yourself – knowledge, communication, body language.

Summary Mind Map® of Chapter 3 – Listening Skills – balancing listening and speaking – the 2:1 ratio, developing listening skills.

Summary Mind Map® of Chapter 4 – Networking – meeting and influencing people – presentation, first and last impressions.

Summary Mind Map® of Chapter 5 – How to Shine in Groups – standing out from the crowd, using your brain to impress – memory, names, conversation.

Summary Mind Map® of Chapter 6 – Confidence Building – relating to others through self-confidence, inspiring confidence – attitudes and behaviour.

Summary Mind Map® of Chapter 7 – Negotiation – resolving conflicts and disagreements amicably – compromise, patience, understanding.

Summary Mind Map® of Chapter 8 – Social Graces – showing care and consideration – thanks, celebrations, gifts, condolences.

Summary Mind Map® of Chapter 9 – Planning a Party – applying what you have learned.

acknowledgements

With profound appreciation to Caroline Shott, my dear friend and literary manager whose vision for and dedication to this new series has inspired everyone who has worked on this project. Especial thanks to my dear friend and Editor-in-Chief, Carole Tonkinson, who has used all ten intelligences to their maximum in her unrivalled dedication to see this precious book through to completion.

Similarly an extra special vote of thanks to my editor, Charlotte Ridings. Charlotte's verbal and spatial intelligences were paramount in helping to sculpt this book into its final form.

Continuing thanks to my extraordinary support team who have now become family. Each one of the following has excelled in their given field and have helped to make the Power of Intelligence series the extraordinary global success that it is becoming: designer Natasha Fidler, Senior Marketing Manager Jo Lal and Publicity Director Meg Slyfield.

A warm welcome to the new member and leader of the team Belinda Budge.

I would also like to thank my home team: Lesley Bias for helping to make the dream come true; my mother Jean Buzan for her ongoing and masterful help in editing, and to Vanda North for her dedication to and help with both this book and the vision of Global Mental Literacy.

chapter one

- Does the thought of walking into a party full of total strangers fill you with dread?
- Does the idea of making small talk with your possible future in-laws leave you a gibbering wreck?
- Have you ever been introduced to a group of people, only to forget their names instantly and flounder for something to say?
- Do you want to make a good impression at a job interview, but are so nervous you can hardly speak?
- Do you wish that you could happily talk to people and make friends easily?

If any of the above scenarios has struck a chord with you, or if your Social Intelligence could do with a bit of a boost, *The Power of Social Intelligence* is designed to help you.

'Social Intelligence' is simply the degree to which we 'get along with' and relate to other people around us. Human beings are, after all, *social* animals, and this ability is absolutely vital if we are to get on in life and enjoy ourselves.

social intelligence – a definition

Almost all of us, if we are being honest, would admit that our 'social skills' could do with a quick polish, and there is a vast range of skills which comprise Social Intelligence.

To begin with, you need to be able to relate to people on a one-to-one basis, in small groups, to a whole roomful of people, and to even larger gatherings. You are involved in Brain-to-Brain communication. The human brain is the most complex, sophisticated and powerful organ in the known universe. To deal with one (your own!) is a hard-enough task. To deal simultaneously with large numbers of other brains successfully is surely a sign of genius!

Socially Intelligent people have to use all of the power of their own brains and bodies to communicate with and to 'read' others. They have to acquire attitudes that encourage others to grow, create, communicate and befriend, and they have to know both how to make and to keep friends!

This massively important intelligence also involves being able to negotiate, as a skilled canoeist does, the rapids of conflict and negotiation situations, mistakes and endings.

All of these skills require that the Socially Intelligent person is a superb conversationalist and listener, able to relate successfully with the wider world. Socially Intelligent people are comfortable with others from different backgrounds, ages, cultures and social strata, and (more importantly) are able to make *those people* feel relaxed and comfortable around them.

Managers need Social Intelligence to do their jobs effectively. So do sales assistants, receptionists, teachers, doctors, social workers, hotel staff … in fact, anyone who deals with any other people at all in the course of their day! Social IQ is one of the most important and beneficial intelligences that we can cultivate – and the good news is, it *can* be cultivated!

social intelligence – strengths and weaknesses

Take a few minutes and jot down on a large sheet of paper the areas of your life where you think that your social strengths and weaknesses lie. Make sure you consider both your home life and your work life – it is amazing how many successful business and professional people find talking to people in a social setting difficult!

Possible areas of your life to think about include:

- Listening to people
- Making social 'small talk'
- Being aware of how other people are feeling
- 'Selling' yourself or your ideas
- Having a positive attitude towards yourself
- Having a positive attitude towards others
- Dealing with awkward or embarrassing situations gracefully
- Building good rapport with people
- Standing out in a crowd – for all the right reasons!

a cautionary tale of social intelligence – part one

When I was a teenager I thought that the way to become popular was to be 'smart' and fit. I went to parties and social events flaunting my high IQ, analysing the faults in others, getting into discussions in which I always tried to prove that my 'opponents' were wrong and I was right, and showing off my good (but rigid!) physique.

Having been told that a high IQ and a fit body were the paths to success, I was taken aback by the number of enemies I was unintentionally making, and the lack of friendship my 'smart/tough/correct' presence was generating.

My realization that simply winning debates was *not* the way to social success was helped along by my father. Once, when I had won the battle – the argument – and lost the war in a social situation, my father gave me a little poem that he said would help me improve my social awareness. The poem went as follows:

> *Here lies the body of Jonathan Grey,*
> *Who died defending his right of way.*
> *He was perfectly right as he sped along*
> *But he's just as dead as if he'd been wrong!*

I began to look around at those who were obviously more socially successful than me. I noticed that they were doing many things that at that time were alien to me, and the opposite of what I had been taught was 'acceptable behaviour' in my school life.

The most popular (and most happy!) people were always smiling and laughing and telling jokes (I 'couldn't'!); they were expressive and open, helpful and considerate of others, and tended to avoid arguments. To make matters even worse for my sensitive teenage soul, they were much more relaxed, much more confident, and much more successful in attracting romance!

Gradually the light began to dawn. My IQ and muscles were not the only strengths I had to develop if I wished to be socially successful: I had to pay attention to the vitally important skills of *understanding* other people – of interpersonal skills – of Social Intelligence.

The Power of Social Intelligence will help save you the trouble of some of those unnecessary experiences I had, and bring you more rapidly the rewards that this amazing Intelligence can bring.

To survive and prosper in the maelstrom of social interactions and life, it is vital to understand and master the intricacies of this incredible intelligence. And it is not only your social life, and that of others around you that will benefit – being successful socially has a fortunate, immediate and positive impact on your wealth, *and* on your physical well being, as the following study reveals.

Want a Cure for Your Colds? Live a Varied Social Life!

Psychologist Sheldon Cohen, of Carnegie Mellon University, has confirmed previous studies that suggest that colleagues, relatives, friends and lovers can act as a 'team' to help protect you from the common cold. Previous studies suggested that people with more active social lives were both healthier and lived longer. Cohen's study has refined this finding, pointing out that it is not simply the absolute number of social contacts that is important; it is their diversity.

Cohen and his colleagues recruited 151 women and 125 men and asked them to keep a record of all the people with whom they had contact at least once every two weeks. As well as the number of

---

people contacted, they were asked also to record the diversity of their social network, breaking down their contacts into 12 categories, including neighbours, colleagues, parents, partners, etc.

The women and men were then exposed to the common cold virus and a record of their rate of infection was also kept.

Of those people with fewer relationships and with restricted social networks, 62 per cent developed colds. However, only 35 per cent of people with relationships from six or more of the categories developed a cold. Cohen theorizes that one of the reasons for the greater immunity is that diverse social networks induced a 'feel-good factor' that boosts the ability of the immune system to attack invading viruses.

the power of social intelligence – an overview

The Power of Social Intelligence is divided into 10 chapters, each one building on the others to help you accelerate the growth of your Social Intelligence as you progress through the book. This chapter, Chapter 1, has given you a quick insight into the importance and potential power of your Social IQ. Here is an overview of the rest of the book.

Chapter 2: Reading People – Body Language and How to Master It

More than half of all communication is through body language. In this chapter I will explain how you project an image of yourself through your body language, and how to read other people through theirs. The human body is a remarkable instrument. It plays the 'music of communication' in very subtle ways. If you learn to play it well, your social rewards will be great.

Chapter 3: The Art of Listening

The most Socially Intelligent people are not the ones who say the most – they are the ones who *listen* the most. In this chapter I will introduce you to the art and science of listening, showing you simple ways in which you can become a master of conversation by saying less!

Remember: you have one mouth and two ears. Think about it!

Chapter 4: Making Connections

It is the natural goal of every human being to want to win friends, to influence people, to be popular, to converse easily, to negotiate with others successfully, and to deal with social relationships in a way that produces the results they desire. Read this chapter and find out how!

Chapter 5: How to Shine in Groups

This chapter will show you how you can stand out from the crowd, and how you can use your brain to impress others at any social gathering!

Chapter 6: 'Attitood' About Attitude

Your attitude profoundly affects not only *your* behaviour, but also the behaviour of others around you, and therefore the behaviour of others with whom *they* interact, and so on in the giant ripple effect that spreads around the entire world. Your own self-confidence is the key to relating with others. I will explain the effects of peer pressure, and reveal one of the most important things that you can give your children.

Chapter 7: Negotiations – How to Win Friends and Influence People

How do you make sure that in any negotiations, *both parties* come away pleased with the outcome? How can you resolve disagreements and conflicts amicably? This chapter will show you everything you need to know!

Chapter 8: Social Graces – Or What to Do When ...

Little gestures that show that you care are immensely Socially Intelligent. This chapter will give you a guide to understanding how such gestures work, and how you can use them for your own benefit and happiness.

Chapter 9: Signposts for Social Success

Developing your Social Intelligence will inevitably give you greater social status and influence. You can apply everything you have learned to guarantee your growing future success. This chapter introduces a

---

great Social Intelligence Star, who is the epitome of the power and qualities of Social Intelligence.

Chapter 10: The 'Power of Ten'

In the final chapter I explain how Social Intelligence is but one among many intelligences we all have, and how each one of your Multiple Intelligence interacts and strengthens all the others.

To help you in your journey, *The Power of Social Intelligence* features a host of apposite quotes, self-check exercises, fascinating stories and case histories. The book also has some special features:

- Mind Maps®. Mind Maps® are amazing thinking tools designed to help you see, outside your head, the 'maps of thought' that are inside your head! Mind Maps® use all the 'equipment' your whole brain uses every day to recognize, understand and remember things, including words, lines, colours and images. Mind Maps® simply make things easier for you wherever and whenever you use them. They are 'Friends of your Brain'.
- Social Workouts. All the following chapters contain a Social Intelligence Workout – games and fun exercises that will help you develop and strengthen this Master Intelligence. You can look on them as your Mental Gymnasium – a place where you go to increase the strength, flexibility and stamina of your Social Intelligence muscles!

■ Social Brain Boosters. These Brain Boosters take the form of Intentions or Affirmations. By repeating them to yourself on a regular basis, you will build up the maps of thought about these intentions in your head, and will increase the probability that what they say will become part of your new social behaviour and growing Social Intelligence. They have been specially designed to protect you from some of the pitfalls of incomplete and inaccurate Positive Thinking modes of thought.

reading people –

body language and how to master it

chapter two

'Use what language you will, you can never say anything but what you are.'

(Ralph Waldo Emerson)

Your body is impeccably designed for the purpose of communicating with your fellow human beings. Your voice and your words obviously play a vital part in the art and science of social interaction. Be fully aware, however, that an even greater percentage of your communication with others is conveyed by – your body. In fact, studies have shown that fully 55 per cent of all meaning conveyed in any act of communication is given by your physical demeanour!

Your body will communicate, without words, whether you are happy or sad, well or unwell, fit or unfit, removed or engaged, confident or nervous, enthusiastic or bored, interested or indifferent, open or defensive, socially ill at ease or socially confident and in command.

And, of course, other people's bodies will communicate the same things to you. If you are aware of this, you will be able to 'read' other people more accurately and empathetically, and so boost your Social Intelligence.

To give you an immediate experience of this, try the following game:

You are to imagine that you are an actor on stage, miming ultimate depression, despondency and despair.

Imagine that you have woken up in the morning to be told by the person you love the most that they find you unutterably grey, boring and dull and wish to have nothing more to do with you. Immediately after this you receive a message that your best friend is gravely ill. This is followed by a phone call from your bank manager informing you that you have just gone bankrupt and will have to sell immediately the house you have lived in and loved for many years.

As you sink into this imaginary total depression, observe what happens to your body. Check the following things:

- **Your diminishing height**
- **Your posture**
- **Your energy levels**
- **Your senses and their lessening alertness**
- **Your breathing and its reduced depth and strength**
- **Your motivational levels**
- **Your desire for social contact**

Now imagine exactly the opposite scenario, one of extreme joy and happiness. Imagine that you have woken up, and the person whom you have secretly loved and desired for many years tells you that they find you the most amazing, attractive, entertaining and wonderful person they have ever met; your gravely ill friend has just had a miraculous recovery; and you have a call informing you that you have just won the Lottery Jackpot.

Now check your posture, energy and motivational levels, the alertness of your senses and your sociability, and feel the difference!

The game you have just played demonstrates how every cell of your body acts as a major communicator to other people. Being aware of this allows you to begin the journey to becoming a master reader of body language. The findings of the game are confirmed in formal studies, like the ones that follow:

Case Study – See and Tell

Psychologists Geoffrey Beattie and Heather Shovelton of the University of Manchester have found that gesture helps convey huge amounts of information. They discovered that when people see storytellers' gestures as well as hearing their voices, they pick up about 10 per cent more accurate information about the story than when they are listening to the voice alone. Beattie and Shovelton say: 'gestures are every bit as rich communicatively as speech; meaning is divided between the hand and the mouth'.

Case Study – Mirror Neurons

An American study has shown that gesture and speech are simply two outlets for identical thought-processes, and both are designed to help you convey those thought-processes to other individuals.

Joanna Iverson, from the University of Missouri, and her colleague Esther Thelen, from the University of Bloomington, Indiana, point to the direct link between movement and meaning that is found in a group of brain cells known as 'mirror neurons', confirmed by a study of monkeys.

The mirror neurons fire both when a monkey makes a particular movement, *and also when it watches another monkey making the same movement.* Intriguingly, these mirror neurons are found in the region of the monkey's brain that exactly corresponds to the speech-production region of the human brain.

who am I?

'If you want to know yourself, see how others behave; if you want to understand others, look in your own heart.'
(Friedrich von Schiller)

The secret of Social Intelligence – to building rapport with others, setting them at ease in your company, making people genuinely glad to be with you, and mixing easily with all types of people – is to 'know yourself'.

If you are comfortable 'being in your skin', you will have inner confidence about yourself, and will know your values and standards. That confidence will radiate out from you, through your body language, and will rub off positively on the people around you.

You can use this Socially Intelligent knowledge to your advantage, even if you are in a situation where confidence is the last thing you are feeling! If you stand with poise and make eye contact, you will exude an aura of confidence. Even better – the more you 'act' confident, the more confident you will find yourself becoming!

However, you should be aware that sometimes the signals you are sending out are not the ones you think you are! An acquaintance discovered that while she *aimed* to project an ultra-feminine and ultra-sexy image, she had no idea that this image was actually interpreted as being overpowering and intimidating!

who are you?

You now know that your body language reveals your true thoughts and feelings, despite yourself. And so, if you become adept at reading other people's body language – sensing whether they are uncomfortable, bored, enthusiastic, upset or worried – you will increase your Social Intelligence multiple-fold.

Studies, like the ones below, have demonstrated that those people able to read body language have many advantages over those who cannot.

Case Study – Read Me, Benefit You!

A Harvard psychologist, Robert Rosenthal, and his students devised a test of people's ability to read non-verbal body signals and language. Rosenthal and his students tested over 7,000 people both in the United States and 18 other countries.

In the tests the subjects were shown a series of videotapes of a young woman expressing a wide range of feelings. The scenes depicted hatred and loathing, a jealous rage, peace and tranquillity, asking forgiveness, motherly love, showing gratitude, and passion.

In all the videos, the sound was muffled so that no speech could be heard. In addition, in each portrayal, one or more of the channels of non-verbal communication had been blanked out. For example, in one the body might be blocked out and only the facial expression shown, in another the facial expressions removed while all bodily gestures remained, and so on.

The results?

A direct correlation was found between being able to read body language and being more sensitive, more well-adjusted emotionally, more outgoing, and, most importantly, more popular.

You will be pleased to learn that this popularity was also directly correlated with success in romantic and sexual relationships!

The success generated by possessing Social Intelligence skills is also reflected in schools. The American Psychological Society reported the results of tests done with 1,011 children that showed that those children who were able to read body language were among the most emotionally stable, did better in academic subjects, and were the most popular.

Understanding body language is of vital importance in social communication. A good friend of mine observed that by playing just three minutes of golf with a new acquaintance, you will learn nearly everything you need to know about that individual, including their ability to accept and learn from success and failure, their generosity, their concern for others, their appreciation of nature, their humour (or lack of it!), how positive/negative they were, their general energy levels, their degree of focus and their honesty.

the secret of social intelligence – smile!

There is a very simple secret to Social Intelligence – smile at people!

A human smile radiates warmth, confidence, a positive attitude, happiness and, very significantly, a welcoming openness to others.

'A man without a smiling face must not open a shop.'

(Chinese proverb)

A simple smile is the best way to win friends and influence people. The thing that first attracts most people to someone else is their smile.

And when we see a smile, our brains trigger our own smiling muscles, so that we smile back!

Brian Bates, co-author of the BBC book and television series *The Human Face*, confirms the importance of smiling in society:

'We would often rather share our confidences, hopes and money with smilers for deep reasons which are often beyond our conscious awareness. Spontaneous smilers have been shown to have a more successful life in personal and career terms.'

Smiles take much less effort than frowns, involve far less muscular tension, and are more instantaneous and spontaneous. The universe even rewards us for smiling! When we smile, the 'smiling reflex' boosts our production of endorphins, the body's natural energizers and pain-killers.

It is now time for your first Social Workout – to be approached with a smile on your face!

social workout

Smile and the World Smiles With You

Recently a witty little poem on smiling appeared on the Internet. I have slightly adjusted it, and recommend that you read it, pass it on, and immediately begin practising what it suggests!

Smiling is infectious; you catch it like the flu,
When someone smiled at me today, I started smiling too.
I passed around the corner and someone saw my grin
And when he smiled I realized I'd passed it on to him.
I thought about that smile and then I realized its worth,
A single smile, one just like mine, could travel round the earth.
So if you feel a smile begin, don't leave it undetected:
Let's start an epidemic quick, and get the world infected!

Smile First

Make sure that you greet people with a smile. People remember first impressions most strongly, so this will be what they remember of you. This is called the Primacy Effect, or the principle of 'First Things First', which we will explore in more detail in Chapter 4. Smiling will get the social interaction off to a positive and uplifting start. You will be gently taking control of the meeting in a 'win-win' way.

Make Your Actions Congruent with Your Words

When you are describing things, allow your body to be the natural musical instrument and artist that it is. Make sounds that mimic what you are describing. With your hands sculpt the objects and scenes you are describing.

Check for Congruence/Incongruence in Others

Check for the congruence between what people's words are saying and what their bodies are saying. You will often find that they are completely opposite. You can practise this Social Intelligence muscle when watching television, especially news and advertisements. Keep a note of some of the more blatant examples of incongruence – they make good conversation pieces themselves!

One extremely amusing instance of incongruent actions occurred when I was at a cocktail party.

I noticed that two businessmen who were supposed to be negotiating with each other were doing an extraordinary dance. Every time one of them moved towards the other, the second almost immediately moved away. It was as if they were two similar poles of a magnet, where the repelling force prevented them from ever making contact. No matter how hard the first tried to get closer, which he was obviously trying to do, the second always moved away. On and on they went, until they had snaked and zig-zagged their way around the entire room!

They were obviously making each other extremely uncomfortable, and not understanding why.

Later on in the evening, I asked them, separately, where they came from. As you might expect, the first one stood very close to me, the second at some considerable distance!

You will not be surprised to learn that the first one came from New York, where closeness to people is part of everyday life, and the second from a vast ranch in Texas, where close contact was very rare.

Being aware of people's different 'comfort zone' is a very important part of Social Intelligence. If you can make people feel comfortable by not invading their personal space, they will immediately be more willing to talk to and spend time with you.

Meeting and Greeting With Feeling

Be particularly alert to body language when you are meeting and greeting people. Remember the two scenarios you imagined before (on page 16) and the extreme positions your body took. Most people will be somewhere between the two.

Once again become the body-language-detective, and quickly assess the many non-verbal messages that are being given during those first vital moments.

If shaking hands, play close attention to the energy of the hand you are shaking – it can speak volumes. In the same way, make sure that your own handshake is firm (not *too* firm!) and welcoming. Make sure you make eye contact with the other person. Brief eye contact acknowledges the other person as being of interest to you – which will make them more interested in you!

Use Appropriate Gestures of Affection

Some cultures use hugs and embraces much more than others. In Russia, for example, hugs are a normal part of greeting people, whereas in Britain, people tend to be more reserved.

Psychiatrist Dr Harold Falk has listed some of the benefits of hugging: 'Hugging can lift depression, enabling the body's immunization system to become tuned up. Hugging breathes fresh life into tired bodies and makes you feel younger and more vibrant.'

In support of this, Helen Colton, author of *The Joy of Touching*, points out that the haemoglobin in your blood increases significantly when you are touched and hugged. As it is the haemoglobin that carries the vital supplies of oxygen to your heart, brain and body, hugging can be seen both as a life-giver and a life-saver, as well as a wonderful expression of Social Intelligence and confidence.

Mirror Talk

Before any social meeting, check yourself – ideally in a full-length mirror. Rather than just casually checking yourself and your appearance, imagine that you are the Costume Director and Producer on a film set. Your function is to make sure that the clothes your star actor (you!) is wearing are perfectly appropriate for the role, and to make sure that your star looks so attractive that other people will actively want to make contact. When you are dressed well and appropriately for the occasion, you and your body feel at ease and confident.

'All the world's a stage ...'

Make a habit of 'people watching'. It is a constant, entertaining, informative (and free!) theatre. Make yourself an increasing expert on the intricate body-language conversations that 'speak to you' on the streets, in restaurants, at social events, on beaches, and in all places where human beings congregate. When you see examples of particularly superb body-to-brain communication, mimic them and incorporate them in your own body language.

social brain boosters

- I am developing my body to be a superb communication device.
- My words and actions are increasingly congruent.
- I am spreading smiles wherever I go.

In the next chapter we will consider another vital non-verbal part of communicating with other people – listening to them!

the art of listening

chapter three

'We are interested in others when they are interested in us.'

(Publilius Syrus)

The Roman poet Publilius obviously knew about Social Intelligence! If someone shows an interest in us and clearly wants to know us better, then we will be more interested and favourably disposed towards them.

The best, easiest and most effective way of showing interest in another person is to *listen* to what they are saying – to *really* listen, focusing on what they are saying, as opposed to standing there planning our own reposts and anecdotes in turn!

Listening in a Socially Intelligent way shows that you find someone to be worth your attention, and to be of value as a person – and everyone responds positively to that.

a cautionary tale of social intelligence – part two

When I was still in the 'Mighty Muscle/Mighty Vocabulary' stage of developing my Social Intelligence, I would tend to 'dominate the airwaves'. This was because I thought that the more brilliant points I made, the more brilliant the conversation was.

This was a very one-sided and limited view.

Nature stepped in and taught me a very valuable lesson.

Just before an important social occasion, I contracted an irritating throat infection. To my chagrin, I could hardly utter a word.

At the party I met someone who was passionate about many things. We began an animated conversation, but because of my weakened voice, I was soon reduced to nodding, massaging the conversation with well-placed 'uhuhms' and very occasionally asking a question, which gave my companion the opportunity to launch into another five-minute conversational journey.

When we eventually parted I assumed that he would consider me an utter bore, as I had contributed probably less than 5 per cent to the conversation, and he comfortably more than 95 per cent.

To my amazement I heard later that he considered me a fascinating conversationalist!

How could this be so?

The light slowly began to dawn: we *had* had a wonderful conversation. He had entertained me with delightful stories and provocative concepts; my body, rather than my voice, had 'spoken back to him', indicating that I was interested, was involved and, by my supportive presence, I had allowed him to explore his own thoughts in good company, and therefore not only to have a conversation with me but also with himself.

I realized that listening gave me this wonderful opportunity to be completely relaxed in a conversation, to be entertained with wonderful tales and thoughts, as well as allowing me to give someone else the opportunity to be freely expressive.

I realized that up to that time, I had been guilty of what Leonardo da Vinci observed: that most people 'listen without hearing'.

This chapter is devoted to helping you listen *with* hearing!

listening — a neglected art

It is estimated that we spend between 50 and 80 per cent of our waking life communicating. On average half of that communication time is spent in listening. In schools and colleges the percentage is even higher, and in the business world listening ranks as one of the top three most important necessary managerial skills. Amazingly, despite all this, listening is the 'poor relation' of communication skills when it comes to being taught, despite the fact that it is learned first and used most, as the table below shows.

Learned	Used	Taught
Listening 1st	Most (45%)	Least
Speaking 2nd	Next most (35%)	Next least
Reading 3rd	Next least (16%)	Next most
Writing 4th	Least (9%)	Most

The Power of Social Intelligence is going to help you redress that balance.

Self-check 1

How would you rate yourself as a listener? On a scale from 0–100, with 0 representing the worst listener imaginable, and 100 meaning that you listen better than anybody else, how well do you think you listen to people?

Self-check 2

On a scale of 0–100, how do you think the following people would rate you as a listener?

1. Your family (you may give them individual ratings or a group average)   _____

2. Your best friend   _____
3. Your other friends   _____
4. Your boss   _____
5. Your work colleagues   _____
6. Any people you supervise at work   _____

Most people (in fact a staggering 85 per cent) rate their listening ability as average or less. On a 0–100 scale, the average rating is 55. Only a tiny 5 per cent score themselves in the 80–90 range, or consider themselves excellent listeners. By the time you have finished reading this chapter, you should be in that top category!

When it comes to other people assessing your listening skills, if you gave your best friend the highest score out of the six groups, you will be in the majority! In fact most people believe that their best friend would give them a higher rating as a listener than they would give to themselves.

People rate their boss as giving them the second-highest listener rating, and this rating also tends to be higher than the rating they give themselves. This is because of the power of authority. People tend to pay more attention to those who have their lives, or part of them, in their hands. Interestingly, and you can muse upon this, colleagues and subordinates tend to be rated exactly the same as the individual rates herself or himself – 55 out of 100.

Scores for family members range widely, depending on the particular structure of the family and the interpersonal relationships. Rather depressingly, the ratings which people thought their spouse or partner would give their listening skills tend to decline in inverse proportion to the number of years they have been together. There is a moral in there ...

bad listening habits

There are 10 listening habits that are most damaging to your skill as a listener and most weakening of your Social Intelligence.

1. Pretending to pay attention when you are really not
2. Trying to do other things while listening
3. Deciding the subject is uninteresting
4. Getting distracted by the speaker's way of speech, or other mannerisms
5. Getting over-involved and thus losing the main thread of the person's argument or thoughts
6. Letting emotion-filled words arouse personal anger and antagonism
7. Concentrating on any distractions instead of what is being said
8. Taking linear, one-colour notes
9. Listening primarily for facts
10. Avoiding anything that is complex or difficult

Of which bad listening habits are you guilty?! Make a note of where your weaknesses lie, and where you can do most to improve your listening skills.

active listening

Listening is *not* a passive activity; it's not the 'unexciting' or 'unflamboyant' part of a conversation. As I myself found out, listening well is the vital ingredient in a successful, productive and interesting conversation.

'Drawing on my fine command of language, I said nothing.'
(Robert Benchley)

Nor is it just a person's words that we should listen to. If we are aware of the other person's body language as well (see Chapter 2) we can intuit so much more meaning from any conversation – we can listen to what they *feel* as well as what they say.

There is a humorous phase that is particularly apt here: 'I know that you believe that you understand what you think I said, but I am not sure you realize that what you heard is not what I meant!'

By listening to the person's whole body, we will in fact 'hear' what he or she meant!

The rest of this chapter is devoted to a Social Workout that will rapidly enhance your listening muscles!

---

social workout

Be Aware of Body Language

Apply what you learned about body language in the previous chapter, and listen to the words that are being spoken *and* to the body language of your conversationalist. This will often tell you as much or more than the words themselves. Listening in this way will make you a 'whole' rather than a 'part' listener.

Be aware of your own body language too. If you are in a slouched, uninterested posture, this will communicate itself to the speaker and will, consciously or unconsciously, depress and demoralize him or her. If you remain alert and body-language-interested, you will communicate to the speaker that you find the conversation interesting, and so will give him or her the confidence to sparkle with more élan.

Your own body-language part in this conversation will also have a significant impact on you and your perceptions. If you are bored, and act bored, your speaker will become even more boring! If you are bored, and act more interested, the speaker will become more interesting. It is you who helps create the dullness or excitement of whatever you are listening to.

Tune-in and Train Your Mind to Focus

You can more easily train your listening skills when you realize what an amazing ability your brain has to focus on specific sounds, and how you do it regularly anyway.

the power of social intelligence

Think about when you are at a party, in a noisy restaurant, in a bar or in a disco. In such circumstances your brain has the ability to completely block out over 50 decibels of thunderous and cacophonous noise as you concentrate on one particular person. You are using the same skill that a mother does when she hears her baby's faint cry above the roar of the madding crowd.

The trick here is to focus on what you want – not what you *don't* want. If you begin to think about how much the distractions are interfering with your concentration, you will magnify them, and they will interfere all the more! If you increasingly focus on who and what you are listening to, you will magnify that sound and fade into nothingness all the background noise.

One easy way to expand your new-found ability to tune-in to sounds is by playing listening games in your daily life. When you are out walking, 'tune-in' to the different 'sound stations' around you. Listen to the bird channel, the human-voice channel, the traffic channel, the rain channel and the breeze-and-wind channel.

Try to isolate only those sounds you want to hear; you will become adept at filtering out unwanted noise. You will gain a much wider and greater appreciation of the surround-sound world in which you live, as well as strengthening your listening skills, and increasing your Social Intelligence.

The 2:1 Ratio

Remember that you have *two* ears and *one* mouth – not the other way round!

Next time you are in an appropriate social situation, try listening for twice as long as you speak. Your Social Intelligence will receive a big boost if you manage this – it is often said that the wiser the person the less they speak and the more they listen.

The Eyes Have It!

Eye contact is such a fundamental part of establishing and showing interest, yet it is often neglected. This is not to say that you have to stare intently into the other person's eyes for the entire course of the conversation (many find this intimidating, although there are obviously occasions when gazing intently into someone's eyes is perfectly acceptable!).

A warm glance every so often will indicate that you are still interested in the conversation, and therefore still interested in the other person.

Mind Map® as You Listen

Many people doodle when they are listening to a talk or presentation, or even when they are on the phone. Rather than being a distraction, doodling actually helps concentration in these circumstances.

A Mind Map® is an organized doodle, which works with your amazing brain's faculties to enable you to remember things far more easily than you would be able to do if you used ordinary, linear note-taking methods.

Mind Maps® are very easy to construct, and there are several wonderful examples given in the colour-plate section of this book. All you need to do is to take a sheet of paper (as large as possible), and draw a central image representing the main subject/idea that you are Mind Mapping.

Imagine that you are listening to a talk on 'The Art of Listening'. This main subject is represented by an image of an ear (see the illustration on page 41). Radiating out from that central image, you would draw some branch-like lines, and print on each an important element of the listening art; for example 'body language', or 'active listening'. From each of these initial branches, you would radiate off others, developing each concept.

The great thing about Mind Maps® is that they use words *and* pictures to create associations in your brain. Not only that, but the more highly original and coloured they are the better. Your multi-faceted, multi-talented brain naturally uses words, colours, shapes and pictures all together. And so you will be working *with* your brilliant brain, rather than against it.

As you build up the interconnected key words, key ideas and key images, your understanding of what you are listening to will soar. Don't worry if your Mind Maps® get a little messy in the process – they probably will! You can easily consider it a rough draft and tidy up your note after the talk or presentation has finished.

Listen With an Open Mind

It is very easy to get distracted by words that trigger negative emotions. Realize that they are, after all, only words, and try to look at them with more objectivity. As you develop your listening skills, you will be able to build up more complete and accurate pictures of other people's internal Mind Maps® of thought. This will enable you to relate to them and to understand them far more fully than if you get tangled up in emotional disagreements.

Use Your Brain Speed

Your brain can think at between four and ten times the speed of speech. This means that when you are listening you have lots of spare time to use your extra 'brain time'. Think 'on your feet', and pay attention to the person's body-language, listening to the meaning between the lines. Organize, summarize, analyse and make Mind Map® notes.

This will make you an active and involved listener – the kind with whom other people love to associate.

Judge Content, Not Delivery

Unless you are a judge in a speaking competition, focus on the content of what is being said. Try not, as many Socially Unintelligent people do, to criticize and negatively judge any inadequacies in delivery and style that the speaker might have. Your negativity will be shown in your body language, which will rub off on the speaker, and will be picked up by others around you. Not the way to win friends and gain contacts.

Remember, concentrate on the content.

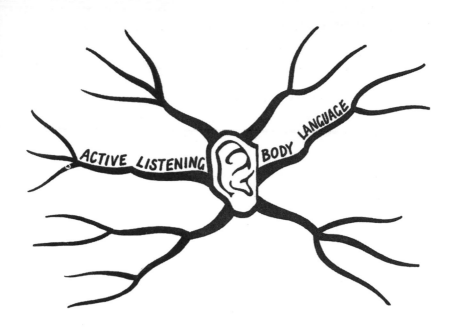

The Art of Listening

Listen For the Big Ideas

Many people listen only for the facts, and end up not being able to see the wood for the trees. Your brain works much more comfortably when it can grasp the overall 'map of the territory', so listen for the big themes for the main branches of your Mind Map®.

When you do this, you will feel more confident and stress free. You will also much more readily be able to slot the facts into their appropriate places, like pieces of a jig-saw puzzle, and so you will understand the conversation much more easily.

social brain boosters

- All my listening skills are improving.
- I am listening with an open mind.
- I am increasingly interested in all subjects.

The next chapter shows how you can put all that you have learned so far about body-language and listening to use, making connections with others.

chapter four

'Only connect!'

(E. M. Forster)

We all know the time and trouble we go to when getting ready for our first date with someone special: the indecision over what to wear (too smart? too casual? too obvious?); the 'do I arrive on time or 10-minutes late' dilemma; the 'what on earth do I talk to him/her about?' anguish; and so on.

However, *every* first meeting really should be approached with the same care – even those unplanned first meetings!

In this chapter I will give you some ideas on how you can make lasting, positive impacts on the people you meet – which will help turn mere acquaintances into real friends, for the benefit of all involved.

The more meetings and interactions you have, the more your Social Intelligence will develop. The wider the circle of friends and acquaintances you will have, the more liked and popular you will become, the more enjoyable life will be, and (believe it or not) the more healthy you will be too!

Case Study – Lonely Hearts

A Swedish study has shown that living alone and having a small network of friends can lead you to an early grave. How? By changing the way your heart responds to everyday stresses.

The study suggests that social isolation is bad for your health, and explains why socially isolated people are more susceptible to heart disease and other illnesses.

Doctor Myriam Horsten and her colleagues at the Karolinska Institute in Stockholm measured the heart rates of 300 healthy women over a 24-hour period. The women were also surveyed about their network of friends and the extent to which they felt angry and depressed.

Horsten and her team were interested in 'heart-rate variability', a measure of how readily a person's heart rate changes over the course of a normal day. A healthy person destined for a long and happy life will have a wide range of heart-rate variation in a 24-hour period. Heart rates that do not vary greatly have been linked to early death, particularly from heart disease.

The findings of the study showed that women who lived alone, with few friends and no-one who could help them with stress-related activities like moving homes, were significantly more likely to have a heart rate with little variation.

Quite obviously, living an active, sociable life will necessarily involve the heart in a wide range of rate-swings. Laughter, excitement, passion, anger, frustration, relaxation and the other vast range of emotions associated with social activities give the heart a wonderful workout that is not the privilege of people living in social isolation.

Concludes Horsten: 'the more social support they have, the higher the heart-rate variability'. She goes on to conclude that living in isolation is a significant risk factor to health and longevity.

first impressions count!

Your brain (and everyone else's) naturally recalls things that it sees or learns first in any given period far better than those it sees or learns later on.

According to this *'First Things First'* Brain Principle, therefore, you will probably remember the first time you met the person who is most important to you at this moment. You will also probably remember the first time you went to a major foreign city or country, and it is highly likely you will remember your first great love affair!

This Brain Principle similarly predicts that when you go to a social event you will be very aware of and will probably recall your first impressions – of the venue, the other people there, and the atmosphere.

And, of course, *so will everyone else.*

Socially Intelligent people are the ones who stand out at first meetings, and are always favourably remembered for their warmth, their positive attitude, and their interest in the other person.

Here are some tips to help you make good first impressions.

- Make sure your body language is positive – stand with poise, confident and alert; shake hands firmly, and look the person in the eye as you say hello with a smile.
- Keep making appropriate eye contact while you are speaking together – it indicates that you find the other person of interest, and that, naturally, makes the other person think that *you* are of interest.
- Act confidently and positively – even if you don't feel it! (Remember Chapter 2.) By acting as if you were relaxed and confident you will make the other person more relaxed, and therefore your own confidence will grow.
- Dress to impress – appropriately! Looking clean and tidy for a job interview is self-evident, but sometimes you need to do a little asking around to find the 'appropriate' look.

last impressions count too!

There is another Brain Principle to go with 'First Things First': that of *'Last Things Too'*. This states that, all other things being equal, you will recall more easily the 'last' things. Check your own memory banks and see if this principle holds for the following.

You will probably recall:

- The last new person you met
- The last time you saw the person you love the most
- The last social event you attended

The Brain Principle *also* predicts that you will not only remember the person or event, but that you will remember where you were, what you were wearing, what the weather was like, who else was with you, what you were talking about and what you were feeling, etc. The principle further predicts that if I asked you to describe in the same detail the 17th similar event, or 35th similar event before that, you wouldn't have the faintest idea!

According to the 'Last Things Too' Principle, you will also remember the following:

- Your last great love affair
- Your last big holiday

- The last meal you had with a friend
- The last time you went to a major foreign town or city

Unfortunately there are millions of people alive today who deeply regret not being aware of this principle. Their last meeting with someone dear or close to them was unpleasant, argumentative or negative; maybe they parted with foul words, insults and invective. And then, for some reason of fate, they were never able to see that person again.

The 'Last Things Too' Principle dooms them to an eternally negative final memory of that person and their social relationship, and often to an eternal regret – had they only known ...

'High-Note' Leaving

Knowing that your social companions will remember, whether they particularly wish to or not, the last moments of your time together, make sure that those moments are uplifting and are 'highlights' for all concerned.

When you leave a friend or acquaintance on an upbeat note, smiling or laughing, being pleasant, giving your heartfelt thanks, and wishing them well, you leave your companion with that long-term memory of your meeting, and of yourself.

In addition you will also give them more physical energy and increase the probability of their long-term health! An uplifting social encounter and departure floods your immune system with 'feel-good' hormones that make your body more resistant to disease – and this works as much for you as it does for them!

So, your Socially Intelligent and altruistic behaviour doesn't just benefit your friends and colleagues; you benefit too. If you leave people on a high note, you leave yourself on that same high note! You thus feed your own memory banks with wonderful and uplifting memories, as well as boosting your own resistance to stress, illness and disease.

BUT REMEMBER: The opposite is also true ...

If you leave your friends, lovers and colleagues on antagonistic and unpleasant notes, you help them to flood their own bodies with poisons that leave them physically unbalanced, their immune systems weakened, and their memories fouled.

And you do the same to yourself!

The choice is yours ...

Saying 'No' and Keeping Friends

Bearing in mind the principle of 'Last Things Too', how then do you say 'no' to people, and still leave them with a positive impression of the encounter?

The trick is to turn people down gracefully and with tact, but with enough assurance that the person realizes that 'no' means 'no', and not 'if you go on at me long enough I'll back down for a quiet life' – whether the request is to work late one night, to go out on a date with someone, or to do an extra turn at the school run.

Make sure that you explain *why* you can't say 'yes' – you're busy, or you've made other arrangements – or, if it's applicable, you simply don't want to: that is your right.

If possible, offer an alternative. You may not want to do the school run tomorrow, but you offer to do it next week – compromise is the key to successful negotiations!

Use your Social Intelligence and show that you understand the reason for your friend or colleague's request, and that you are sorry that you cannot help out. A sympathetic rejection, which demonstrates concern for the individual, is almost always remembered more fondly than a brusque acceptance, which gives the impression of thoughtlessness.

the art of conversation

The aim of conversation is to establish a connection with another person, to exchange ideas and information with them, and, above all, to make them feel that they matter and are special. Thanks to your ever-expanding Social Intelligence, you now know that if you make someone feel important, they will automatically be more friendly and helpful towards you.

Conversations come in all sorts of shapes and sizes – from casual chats with friends and social small talk at parties, to work-related talks with your boss. Some people can hold formal work conversations without any problem, but 'dry up' when it comes to polite small talk with strangers. Still others are quite happy chatting away, one-to-one, but dread the thought of speaking to a group.

Below are some tips and pointers to help you make all your conversations Socially Intelligent, productive and beneficial to everyone concerned. I will look at how you can present yourself in the best light possible to a new acquaintance, how to network, and how to overcome the fear of saying the wrong thing at the wrong time.

Small Talk – Big Rewards

'In the room the women come and go talking of Michelangelo.'
(T.S. Eliot)

People often find making 'small talk' at social gatherings very nerve-wracking. They worry that they will have nothing interesting to say, that the other person will think them dull and boring, and that the 'conversation' will grind to a stop in awkward silence.

The following hints will ensure that you will never be stuck for something to say at a party!

Plan ahead and keep informed

Try reading the weekend papers' arts pages or the sports reviews. They will give you a mine of new topics to talk about, and will ensure that if the conversation turns to the latest tennis grand-slam prospects, or the current 'must-see' film or exhibition, you will be able to respond knowledgably and with enthusiasm.

In the same way, if you know that a particular person is going to be at the event, try finding out from mutual friends what his or her interests are, so you can read up on them beforehand!

Keep some anecdotes handy

Telling humorous anecdotes and stories is a great way to keep a conversation going. Holidays and travels are marvellous sources for these, and the more unusual, outstanding and funny you can make them, the better.

Not only does humour demonstrate Social Intelligence, our brains are hard-wired for humour, as the following case study shows.

Case Study – Seeing the Funny Side of Things

Research in Toronto done by Dr Donald Stuss of the Rotman Research Institute examined an area of the brain the size of a billiard ball in the upper front part of the brain, known as the right or medial prefrontal cortex.

Stuss and his colleagues showed that this part of the brain was intimately involved in understanding jokes, detecting cheating, and understanding the mental processes of others so that we can feel empathy and sympathy; it also helps us understand humour, enabling us to distinguish when others are being, ironic, sarcastic or even deceptive.

It appears that the brain has been *designed* to help us interact on both simple and complex levels with our human companions.

Keeping the conversation flowing

A conversation can be compared to a two-person relay race: the first person picks up the conversation and runs with it as far as he or she can, and then passes it over to the other 'stage runner', who takes the conversation as far as possible, before handing it back again.

If both runners contribute equally to the conversation, then they will be able to keep going with it for a long time, because they will both get enough 'rest' between their stages. If, however, one of the conversationalists only takes the topic on a little way before passing the baton back, the second person will get tired quickly and will eventually stop running.

The secret of flowing conversations is to ask 'open' questions – those that need a longer answer than 'yes' or 'no' – and to reply giving colour and detail.

For instance, you are asked where you went on holiday this year. You could answer that (for example) you went to Malta for a couple of weeks. Alternatively, you could reply that you spent a couple of weeks in Malta, hiring a car for a week to travel round the island, seeing the old towns and crusader bases. Then you spent the second week relaxing in one of the small, colourful fishing villages, soaking up the sun and atmosphere. You can then ask your conversation partner if *they* have ever been to Malta.

If the other person is as Socially Intelligent as you, their reply will probably either be on the lines of yes, they've also been to Malta, and especially enjoyed the beaches/harbours/good weather/local architecture; or no, they haven't been to Malta, but they have been to

Crete/Cyprus/Italy/Greece and ...

In this way, the conversation ping-pongs between the two of you.

Listen!

One big fear many people have at parties and social gatherings is of being boring. They wrongly think that they do not have an interesting life or opinions to talk about.

If this worries you – don't let it. Look back at the previous chapter and brush up your listening skills. Only one of you can talk at a time, and the more sympathetic and intelligent listener you are, the more the other person will talk to you.

Remember the ears:mouth ratio!

Fitting Conversations

The mark of people with high degrees of Social Intelligence is their ability to converse readily and easily with all sorts of people in all sorts of situations.

It doesn't matter if the conversation is a brief passing the time of day with the person behind the counter at the local grocery store, a discussion of your car's problems with the garage mechanic, or an appraisal review with your boss – the principles behind Socially Intelligent conversations are the same.

- Always show respect for the other person. Never talk down to others. Try to speak to everyone in the same way in which *you* would like to be addressed.
- Be aware of what you want to come away from the conversation having achieved – a friendly exchange of gossip and news; reassurance that your car will be fixed; an honest discussion of work targets, future goals and your performance.
- Use language that is appropriate to the particular situation. For example, your chat with the grocer will be casual and friendly in tone; the mechanic needs to know precise facts about what the car is or is not doing – i.e., it is tending to veer to one side of the road – maybe the wheels are out of alignment; your boss will appreciate a professional, business-like conversation about your work, complete with supporting evidence of your performance against any set targets.

Presentations

Group talks or presentations are best seen as conversations with several people at once, for although normally people won't contribute responses during your period of speaking, you will certainly be receiving feedback and encouragement from them via their body language and general reactions to what you are saying (laughter, murmurings of agreement or disagreement, etc.).

Remember the brain principles of 'First Things First' and 'Last Things Too' (pages 46–49)? You can use this knowledge to make sure that whatever you wish the group to remember from your talk is far

Summary Mind-Map® of Chapter 2

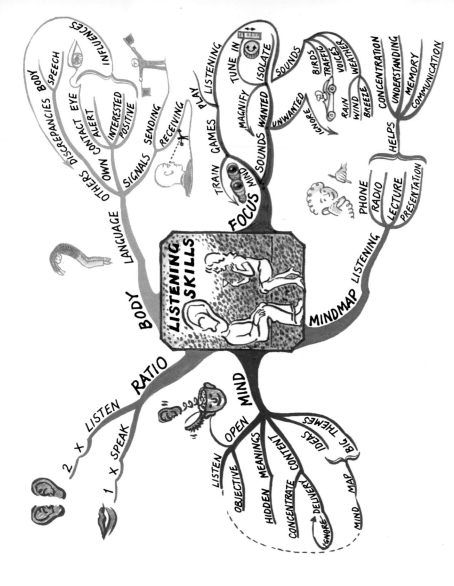

Summary Mind-Map® of Chapter 4

Summary Mind-Map® of Chapter 5

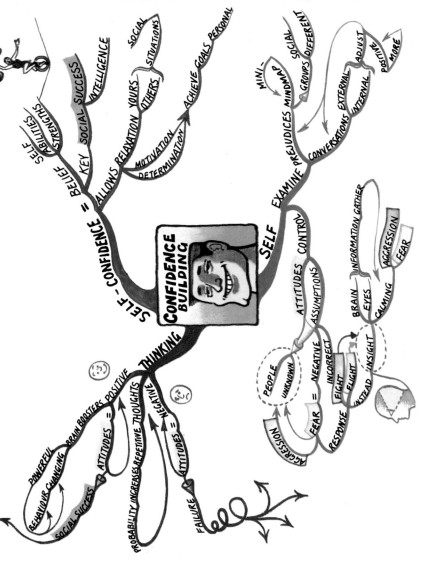

Summary Mind-Map® of Chapter 7

Summary Mind-Map® of Chapter 8

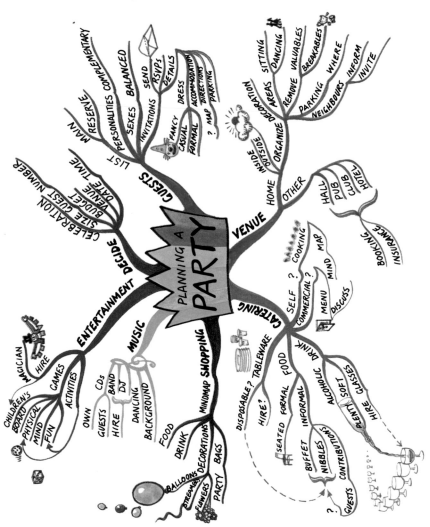

more likely to be remembered. Human brains remember things that occur at the beginnings and endings of sequences better than those that happen in the middle. Make sure you put your most important points at the beginning and end of your talk. (This, of course, applies for any and all conversations.)

Make your important points outstanding, and therefore memorable, in some way – use outrageous, imaginative stories to add emphasis.

Planning your speech beforehand using Mind Maps® will help you calm those nerves, and enable you to relax and give a brilliant, witty, memorable and Socially Intelligent talk.

Presenting Yourself

**' … there will be time
to prepare a face to meet the faces that you meet.'**

(T.S. Eliot)

Self-presentation is the same as marketing yourself, and it should be regarded in just the same way as if you were trying to sell any sort of product – a car, a holiday or even a box of cornflakes! The only difference is that the 'product' is *you!*

You have to make yourself attractive to the 'buyers' (the people that you are trying to impress or get to know), so that they will take an interest in you. You have to make sure that you stand out from all the other competing 'products' on the market – to have what marketing people call a USP, or 'Unique Selling Point'. This 'outstanding' principle (which is known as the von Restorff Effect) is examined in more detail in the next chapter (see page 67). But one story here will show how it works, and how important it is.

A Socially Intelligent IBM computer salesman decided to use the von Restorff Effect to help him be a great success in his chosen career. As IBM was known as Big Blue, he decided to take that colour and to 'von Restorff' himself by using the colour blue.

He bought himself a new wardrobe consisting only of blue shirts, suits, ties and coats. He bought himself a blue car with blue upholstery, a blue-faced watch with a blue strap and a blue briefcase. He designed his own light-blue letterhead, and had a blue fountain pen containing blue ink.

Everywhere he went he stood out as a unique character. He became known as 'Mr Blue' and because of his total dedication to his identity, his job, his uniqueness and his customers, rapidly became one of IBM's top salesmen.

Because 'Mr Blue' was so unique people wanted to associate with him, and therefore gave him their custom. He had made himself stand out in the memories of his customers in the same way that he probably stands out in your memory now!

Above all, you have to know what it is you are 'selling', and to believe in the 'product' – i.e., you have to have confidence in yourself and your own abilities.

Networking

Networking is really part of self-presentation – and Socially Intelligent people tend to do it automatically.

All it involves is making connections with the people that you meet. You should approach everyone you meet as someone potentially important in your life – which, of course, they are. If someone is important to you, you tend to make sure that you treat that person with respect and value his or her friendship.

This is as true of the friend of a friend you meet casually as it is for an encounter in a more formal setting in circumstances more 'obviously' designed for business/social/career networking – at a conference or talk for example.

The Fear of 'Getting it Wrong'

One of the biggest fears people have is of saying the wrong thing, at the wrong time, and of being rebuffed by the other person.

For example, you ring a friend for a chat, only to have your friend turn round and say, curtly, that he or she can't talk now, and ring off. Naturally, you are put out and hurt.

However, with your growing and developing Social Intelligence, you will by now know how you can deal with such a situation. *Don't take it personally!*

Put yourself in the other person's shoes and realize that, to take the first example above, your friend may be rushed off his or her feet: the baby is running a fever, the boss has just dumped a load of work on their desk with a totally unreasonable deadline, the doorbell has just rung ... No wonder they don't want to stop and chat!

The Socially Intelligent approach is to ask at once whether it is a good time to talk. Your friend will appreciate your thoughtfulness, and you will get a much warmer reply in turn. And, when they do ring back, you will both enjoy a far more relaxed, friendly conversation!

You are ready to connect with your Social Workout!

social workout

Become a Good Greeter!

There are many complex formulas for the different manner in which you should greet your friends/boss/associates/business contacts/new acquaintances, etc. These become less necessary when you know the basic formula for all meeting situations:

1. Enter the greeting situation positively and optimistically.
2. Smile.
3. Shake hands/hug warmly and with open body-language.
4. Start the 'proceedings' with matters that relate, not to you, but to *them*.
5. You've already won!

Make Your Smile Your Signature!

From the body-language chapter (Chapter 2) you already know that your smile has the power to transform. This is especially true in close and professional relationships. Constantly bear this in mind, and *make your smile your signature*.

Become Genuinely Interested in Other People

There is no one as interesting as someone who is interested in you! The important, Socially Intelligent word is 'genuine'. When you are genuinely interested, all your body-language signals will speak the truth of your interest. If you fake it, your own body will expose you!

You can become genuinely more interested in people by making them your hobby and by realizing how incredibly unique each individual is.

Make Sure You Leave on a High Note

Make your leavings pleasantly memorable for all concerned. Use your new awareness of the 'Last Things Too' principle to make your goodbyes count.

Try not to part on hastily or on bad terms with anyone. You do not know when, or if, you will see them again.

Get a Vision! Get a Social Life!

If you have no main purpose in life at the moment, work on defining one. Make a note, ideally in Mind Map® form, of all your interests.

Then think what you would like to accomplish personally in the next five or ten years, and in your life as a whole.

Remember that goals and visions can change as your life progresses. It is important, simply, to decide on one. Common life visions include:

- Travelling the world
- Being the best mum/dad/family member I can be
- Mastering some musical, physical or academic skill or subject
- Being my own boss
- Making as many people happy as I possibly can

Once you have decided on your dream, support yourself in your decision. Read books, check the Internet, join clubs and go to social functions that will help you realize your goal. As you do this you will automatically be expanding your circle of friends and contacts.

Practise Your Conversation Skills

Strike up conversations with the people you meet as you go about your life. Exchanging a few words with shop assistants every day will give you good practice and help build your confidence if you are still unsure about talking to people you don't know. Try 'putting yourself into others' shoes'-type conversations (see page 59), and see how well people respond and warm to you.

Learn to Laugh at Yourself

If you can laugh, the world *will* laugh with you. If you can laugh at yourself, the world will laugh even *louder* with you! Being able to laugh at yourself shows that you have the ability to step outside yourself and to see things from many different perspectives. It also indicates that you are not taking yourself too seriously all the time - a death knell to relationships if you do. Laughing at yourself will also increase your ratio of smiles ...

Mind Map® Talks and Conversations

If you are facing a more formal conversation or presentation, make sure you Mind Map® what you wish to say beforehand. This will make your conversation more logical (very important in a business situation). You will also remember all the apposite points you wish to make.

social brain boosters

- I am applying the 'Last and First' Principles to improving the social lives of others and myself.
- I am increasingly making sure that my body language reflects the words I am speaking.
- I am applying the von Restorff Principle to my communication, memory and life!
- I am increasingly interested in the personal history and life of every unique individual I meet.
- My increasingly clear life vision assists me in the development of my Social Intelligence.
- My sense of humour is becoming increasingly pleasant and playful.

chapter five

Many, many people, even those who are confident and sociable on a one-to-one basis, curl up and die when it comes to attending large gatherings or parties. The sea of strange faces overwhelms them, and they spend most of the time standing in a corner desperately trying to recognize at least one friendly face to approach. Eventually they manage to escape, and miserably vow never to attend such an event again!

However, imagine an alternative scenario ...

Our partygoers enter a room confidently, looking round to size up the crowd. They then wander over to join a group they like the look of, listen to the conversation for a few minutes, and then gradually add the odd friendly, neutral comment of their own. Introductions are made, and after a little while they are at the heart of the group.

This can be repeated as often as necessary – if one group is too well established and close knit to allow a 'stranger' in, then our Socially Intelligent partygoer moves on to another group.

This chapter contains hints and tips to help you enjoy social events and occasions, rather than merely endure them.

working the crowd

As with most things, there is a trick to working a crowded room, which can be learned, practised and developed.

First (and you've heard this before): ACT CONFIDENTLY.

If you think 'Help, I don't know anyone. I don't want to be here!' you aren't going to project a very positive image to the rest of the people there. If, however, you mentally take a deep breath before you plunge in, you will look and feel instantly more confident, positive and at home. You will be able to calm your nerves better, and the calmer and more relaxed you appear, the more relaxed other people will be when meeting you. You create a positive spiral.

The next thing to remember is that crowds are made up of individuals. There is bound to be at least one other person there who is wandering round looking a little lost. Approach them with a smile and sympathetic body language, and introduce yourself. They will almost certainly be so pleased that *you* have taken an interest in them, that *they* will be interested and well-disposed towards you.

If you can't spot anyone on his or her own, head for any buffet or food table. It is very easy to make conversation with people over the canapés. Better still, you could take a tray of something round the room – this is an infallible way of breaking the ice.

Remember to use your body-language reading and listening skills to the full. Before you know it you will have relaxed, settled down and found yourself enjoying the party.

the association principle

One of the hardest things people often find at social gatherings, is remembering people's names when they are introduced. This is especially true when you are introduced to a number of people at once, and you are already nervous.

The Association Brain Principle says that to be fit mentally, physically and socially you need to *associate*. If you wish to learn well, you have to make the right connections between things; if you wish to remember well, you have to create vivid associations between things you already remember and the new things you wish to remember; if you wish to be socially skilled or a social leader, then the more successful associations you need to make with other people.

There is a corresponding Brain Principle to that of Association – the von Restorff Effect, or the 'Outstanding' or 'Memorable Principle'.

In the early part of the 20th century, a certain Dr von Restorff performed a series of experiments that provided interesting findings for those wishing to develop their Social Intelligences.

Von Restorff's amazing discovery was that we tend to remember those things, people, places, etc, which we associate in our brains as *outstandingly different*.

Is this true for you?

Let's check it.

Von Restorff's Principle predicts that when you are reminiscing with your friends about the good times and your past memories, you will regularly say things such as 'Do you remember that *most incredible* week we all spent skiing in the Alps?', or 'Wasn't that the *most fantastic,* electrifying goal you have ever seen?', or 'I have never seen a *more glorious* sunset than the one we saw together in the summer of 2001', etc.

Here is a quick quiz to check this Principle. Below is a list of cities and countries. The second you read the city/country, note down the first building that pops as an image into your mind.

There are obviously tens of millions of buildings from which you could choose. Von Restorff's Principle, however, predicts that 99 out of 100 people will give the same answers!

Here are the countries and cities:

1. Egypt
2. India
3. Paris, France
4. Rome, Italy
5. Athens, Greece
6. London, England
7. Sydney, Australia

Here are the answers given by most other people who have done this quiz – how do your answers compare?

1. Egypt   The pyramids
2. India   The Taj Mahal
3. Paris   The Eiffel Tower (Notre Dame and the Louvre occasionally mentioned)
4. Rome   The Coliseum
5. Athens   The Parthenon
6. London   Big Ben (St Paul's occasionally mentioned)
7. Sydney   The Opera House

Von Restorff rules!

Understanding this vital human principle gives you tremendous insight into other people and our social behaviour.

Because we all naturally wish to be remembered by friends, colleagues and others in general, we all naturally try to make sure that in some way we *stand out* in other people's memories. Remember the story of 'Mr Blue' in the previous chapter? He certainly made sure that he stood out.

Remember Them?!

One of the greatest boosters to your social self-confidence and popularity, is to remember the names of the people you meet. This is much easier if you can find out something outstanding about them. Ask them about the most exciting things that ever happened to them;

their main purpose for living; the most beautiful thing they have ever seen; their most memorable event, etc. This will give you an outstanding von Restorff image, which you can then combine with the Association Principle to help you connect their name to their von Restorff 'effect'.

A bonus of this is that your showing an interest in other people's 'mosts' will make them warm towards you, as well as providing you with some extremely engaging social conversations.

Alternatively, you can use the Association and von Restorff's Principles to link your new friend's name and appearance together irrevocably in your mind. Conjure up the most outrageous, over-the-top, outstanding image of your acquaintance, linking something about his or her general appearance and name – the more outlandish the better. Your brain will 'von Restorff' the image, and you will be easily able to recall who they are if you meet them again later. For example, if you meet Daisy Hill, you would imagine her sitting on top of a magnificent hill festooned with brilliantly white daisies.

stand out from the crowd

If you wish to be remembered in social gatherings, or business meetings, in job interviews, or if you have to give any sort of presentation, you now know how to do it! Take the example of Mr Blue and dress or present yourself in a way that makes you, to your own comfort, slightly or significantly different from the crowd. Alternatively, you can start developing unique interests and hobbies, which will (of course) help widen your circle of friends and acquaintances!

If you shine out from everyone else you *will* be remembered.

There is, of course, another side to shining among groups of strangers – bringing interesting mixes of people together.

the art of bringing people together

The secret of organizing any successful gathering is planning, planning, planning. Mind Maps® (see Chapter 3) are wonderful tools to use for this, and there is an example of a Mind Map® around the theme of planning a party in the colour-plate section.

Learn to spot when guests are ill at ease, and how to make them relaxed and comfortable at your gathering. Simple little things that make people feel ill at ease are often overlooked in social situations. These include: feeling cold; feeling thirsty; feeling hungry; needing to go to the bathroom; feeling ill; not knowing what's going on; not knowing anyone else in the gathering; and worrying about some personal problem. Be aware of these issues, especially at the beginning of the event (the primacy effect applies here, too!).

All except the last are easily solvable, but you have to be aware of the problem first. Your empathizing and body-language reading skills should come to the fore here.

The Socially Intelligent host makes sure that the guests will complement each other, and will draw out the quieter ones by astute introductions, if need be – especially if the majority of people at the event already know each other, while there are one or two others who know only you.

The atmosphere is also very important to any occasion. When you are hosting or organizing social events, make sure that your events appeal to all the senses. Make sure that the environment is visually appealing, has sounds and music that are appropriate to your guests, has aromas and fragrances that fit and create the moods you desire, has foods that delight the palate, and has textures that appeal to the touch.

Your guests will be able to relax and enjoy themselves, and you will have planned and executed a super-successful, memorable social event!

social workout

Mind Map® your Friends, Colleagues and Customers

Socially successful people have an intimate knowledge of their friends, colleagues, customers and acquaintances. They invariably keep detailed records of the most important people in their lives.

The Mind Map® is an ideal tool for doing this. When you meet a new person whom you think will be significant in your life, put a little image in the centre of a page that summarizes his or her character, personality, life or physical features. Radiate some main 'branches' from this central image, representing such main 'chapter headings' as: Family; Occupation; Interests; Physical Appearance ('distinguishing features'); History; Characteristics, etc. From each of these main branches you can expand your themes, giving you a complete and growing picture of that person.

This is an excellent memory tool for recalling acquaintances and business associates whom you meet again later. They will be very impressed by your detailed recall of your previous meeting.

Listen!

It is easy to use your listening skills to make an impression at gatherings – especially if you are not confident enough yet to dazzle total strangers with your wit and conversation.

Remember the story of my lost voice in Chapter 3?

Listening to other people makes them feel important. When you make people feel important, you are making *them* a von Restorff, and everyone loves to be a von Restorff! They will appreciate an audience, and naturally think that you are a special person to appreciate them.

Put People at Their Ease

Be aware of those things that can make people feel uncomfortable – being too hot, too cold, etc. If you ask them if they are comfortable at the start of your meeting, you will demonstrate what a thoughtful, caring person you are.

If you look after people in this way, you will become known as a warm, compassionate and desirable friend and companion.

Mind Map® Social Events

When you are planning meetings, celebrations, weddings, birthdays and parties, Mind Map® them.

On the Mind Map® make sure you consider all the big and little things that are important to the social event's success. Such a Mind Map® gives you the 'whole picture' of the event; makes you feel more confident and in control; and is a lot more fun than the deadly dull list which often gets out of control, and which buries within it the nagging feeling that something important may have been missed out – which it often has been!

Mind Mapping an event also encourages you to be more creative in your planning. This will lead to a more memorable party, and your rapid ascent up the Social Intelligence ladder!

Hone Your Association Skills

Practise associating people's faces, names, characters and interests with as many outlandish images that you can think up. You will find your memory, creativity and recall expanding by leaps and bounds. And it is fun to do!

social brain boosters

- I am enhancing my powers of Association.
- I am an increasingly outstanding example of von Restorff's Principle.
- I am increasingly empathetic towards others.
- I am developing my senses.

In the next chapter I look at how our attitudes affect our social relations, and how we can cultivate a positive outlook on life.

'attitood' about attitude

chapter six

'If you think you can or can't, you're always right.'

(Henry Ford)

Can one's own personal attitude really have a significant effect on social success? 'Surely not!' echo a chorus of many voices.

'Surely it can!' echo the great thinkers, and an increasing array of studies.

To find out how personal attitude can mean the difference between *complete* failure and *complete* success, read on.

the tale of the two seekers-of-truth

This tale comes from Eastern folklore. Two students seeking spiritual enlightenment were travelling the same spiritual and, coincidentally, physical path.

The first student stayed at a small village overnight, and set out early next day on the long trek to the next village, which was over 30 miles away.

On his way he met an ancient wise man and plied him with questions about the meaning of Life, the Universe and Everything. The wise man patiently and carefully answered every question the young man posed.

At the end of his questioning, the young man thanked his elder and asked if he was heading in the right direction for the next village, and whether the old guru knew the people of the next village, and if so what they were like.

The guru confirmed that the young man was headed in the right direction, and before answering his second question, he asked what the people in the village the student had just visited were like. The student said that they were extraordinary. Although poor, when he had entered the village they had greeted him warmly and openly, had offered him a free night's board in their own homes, and had generously fed him, without charge, from their meagre rations. He marvelled at their kindness, civility, openness and generosity.

'I have some good news for you,' said the guru. 'The people in the village to which you are going are exactly the same. Enjoy your journey and enjoy them!'

Coincidentally the second student, on the following day, stayed in the same village that the first student had just left. The next morning he too set out on the same path.

Halfway to the next village, he met the same guru, and similarly plied him with questions. At the end of his questioning he also asked the guru if he were on the right track for the next village, and what he might expect from the people there.

The guru confirmed to him that he was on the right track, and, just as he had done the day before, he asked the young man to describe the people in the village he had just left.

'I was amazed,' said the young man. 'They were as surly and unfriendly a bunch as you could expect to meet. Although I was tired and hungry they offered me little support and no friendship. When I insisted on a place to stay, they said there was none, so I had to make do sleeping in a nearby field. They churlishly told me that they had little enough food for themselves, so had none to spare for me. I found them brutish and foul. I hope never to see them again.'

'Sadly, young man,' said the guru, 'I have some bad news for you: you will find the people in the next village just as bad as those you left. Try to enjoy your journey and learn what lessons you can.'

What kind of student are you ...? What kind of student are you in the process of becoming?!

A positive outlook works wonders for your social success, and Socially Intelligent people make sure that they always 'look on the bright side of life'.

'Most folks are about as happy as they make up their minds to be.'
(Abraham Lincoln)

bad attitood

Mimicking and Peer Pressure

One of the great abilities your brain is endowed with is the ability to copy: to mimic. This phenomenal ability, almost infinite in its application, is one of the best ways of learning anything. In fact, mimicking is a fundamental principle of nature (it is how young creatures learn how to survive), and this necessary need to copy explains a vast amount of our social attitudes and behaviour.

Sports-mad youngsters avidly try to copy their heroes; teenagers emulate their pop idols; and all the great athletic and sporting champions say that they were inspired by the previous great champions, in whose footsteps they wanted to follow.

Why? What is it about these heroes and heroines that attracts others?

It is their qualities and success which makes youngsters (and not so youngsters!) want to copy, or mimic them – in order to be as equally successful. The list of useful things to copy and want to be includes:

- Energy
- Wealth
- Fame
- Power
- Sexual desirability
- World travel
- Accomplishment
- Independence
- Freedom
- Social power
- Leadership

The importance of setting a good example is wonderfully illustrated in the study below, of the behaviour of young children being driven by their parents.

Back-seat Mimickers

If you are a good and careful driver your children will probably be good and careful drivers too. Conversely, if you are a menace behind the wheel, then your children will probably also turn out to be menaces!

In North Carolina, Susan Ferguson, of the Insurance Institute for Highway Safety, and her colleagues checked the accident records of 140,000 families. They then compared the records of parents and their children when the children were between the ages of 18 and 21.

Their findings revealed that the children of parents who had been in at least three crashes in the previous five years were 22 per cent more likely to have crashed in turn than the children of parents who had not had any accidents in the same time period.

The findings also revealed further 'mimicking behaviour': traffic violations such as exceeding the speed limit and running red lights were also correlated. If the parents had three or more violations, the children were 38 per cent more likely to have broken traffic laws too. These findings were substantiated by Jane Eason, the spokeswoman for the UK's Royal Society for the Prevention of Accidents: 'If parents set a bad example, it is logical that the child will follow suit.'

Because we naturally tend to copy 'best behaviours', the more we can set a good example, the more other people will follow that example. Of course, the Brain Principle of mimicking has its downside – copying behaviour, attitudes and beliefs in order to 'fit in' and to 'conform'.

The power of peer pressure is clearly demonstrated in this next story of a study with which I was involved.

A Fascinating Social Experiment

I was asked to help in an experiment on human behaviour, to show the incredible and unknown power each of us has over others. The experiment was originally designed by an insightful investigator of human social interaction by the name of Professor Asche. It was performed as follows:

Picture a small, fairly bare room. At the front is a plain desk with one chair behind it. About 10 feet in front of the desk, and facing it, is a row of three chairs. The whole arrangement is much like a mini-theatre. There is nothing else in the room. The experiment involved five people: two 'psychologists' in 'official' white scientific coats, and three observers.

In the experiment, one of the 'psychologists' stood and presented 'visual tests' to the observers, while the other 'psychologist' recorded the results and described the experiment to the observers. My role was as the recorder, who also had to describe the experiment to the observers. This is what I had to say to the three students:

'You are going to be shown a number of cards. On each card there will be three vertical black bars. Each bar will be labelled "A", "B" or "C" at the top of it. Your task is to state, in order, the letter of the tallest, middle and shortest bar. The order of the bars on each card will vary throughout. The person to the left will always go first, the person in the middle second and the person on the right, last.'

A B C

However, there was a mischievous twist to the plot! Unknown to the observer sitting on the right, the other two observers were in on the experiment! The cards had been especially arranged and the two false observers had both rehearsed giving predetermined incorrect responses as they dramatically acted out their 'thinking processes'.

To the first two cards presented, both 'One' and 'Two' shot back the correct answers. To the third card 'One', with a mix of correct and incorrect responses, feigned anguish but eventually stated that the medium was the tallest, the tallest the medium and the shortest, the shortest. 'Two' ummed and ahhhed on cue, rocked back and forward in his chair, voiced his indecision, and then finally decided 'yes, yes I agree ...': and gave the same answers as 'One'.

You can guess the state of mind of poor 'Number Three', and imagine how you would react in that situation.

This procedure was repeated for a total of 17 cards. 'One' increasingly giving more wrong answers, and 'Two' always agonizing before agreeing with him when he was wrong. On the rare occasions when 'One' answered correctly and immediately, 'Two' always

the power of social intelligence

responded with similar conviction and speed.

We repeated this same experiment with 20 different 'Number Threes', conscientiously recording all their responses. What do you think they were?

Do you think they all disagreed with 'One' and 'Two'? Do you think some of them did? Do you think none of them did?

The results were stunning, shook me to the core, and made me realize for the first time in my life just how powerful our social influence over each other truly is.

Over 60 per cent of 'Threes' totally agreed with everything that the misleading numbers 'One' and 'Two' said! When the 'Threes' were retested on the same cards in isolation, they scored 100 per cent accuracy. When confronted with their test results and asked to explain the discrepancies, they said that they had physically seen the correct relationships. They had, however, been so persuaded by the responses of numbers 'One' and 'Two' that they felt they must have somehow been wrong in what they saw and so decided to 'go along with the crowd'.

Astonishingly, a small percentage of this 'agreeing group', when confronted with their two massively different results on the same tests, said that they had 'called it as I saw it'! This suggests that the power of social interaction is so great that it can actually completely distort our perceptions.

Even those rugged individualists who stuck to their true perceptions against the socially persuasive power of 'One' and 'Two', went through either agonies or violent emotions. One individual began increasingly

---

to look quizzically at the others, and in the later tests took out his comb and measured the bars much like an artist measuring for a picture!

Another, when number 'One' stated flatly the shortest was the longest and the longest the shortest on one card, exploded in fury at him, exclaiming 'What's the matter with you, you idiot, can't you SEE?'

Asche's experiment, which has been repeated thousands of times with similar results, underlines the fact that even basic social interactions have the power to produce in us strong emotions, to make us consider our own truths doubtful, and even to change the very way in which we see – not to mention demonstrating the hold social conformity has over us!

Stereotyping Stereotypes

One phenomenon that springs from our natural desire to fit in and conform, is that of generalizing, or stereotyping others: *girls are no good at science; boys are aggressive; Asians are hardworking; old people are always complaining; Mediterraneans are lazy;* and so on and so on.

Stereotypes and prejudice arise because by nature (and, unfortunately, often by upbringing), we tend to feel more relaxed and comfortable around people who are similar to us – in looks, attitudes and outlook on life. We tend to fear the unfamiliar and unknown.

But stereotyping breaks one of the fundamental 'laws' of Social Intelligence – to treat each person as a unique individual, worthy of respect.

Flight! Fight! Insight!

Stereotypes are caused by ignorance. As humans, our first response to the unknown is fear and trepidation – which then go on to trigger our primal 'flight or fight response'. What your brain is actually doing is giving you a 'first take', in accurate and general terms, of a new person. Depending on the associations you have with that general type, you will decide on either the 'flight or fight' response.

This 'flight or fight response' is to anything that is different in your environment – from people of different races, to women entering social clubs and venues that are normally frequented by men.

The mistake we often make is to take our brain's accurate observation and natural response, and add incorrect attitudes and assumptions, which make us immediately aggressive or afraid.

Now that you are much more developed in your Social Intelligence, you can move to the next stage of this natural equation: the *'Flight! Fight! Insight!'* response.

Next time someone unfamiliar triggers your instinctive 'flight or fight response' add, consciously, the Socially Intelligent and superior response of *insight*. This means: pause, and allow your eyes and brain to gather as much data about the individual as you possibly can in the time you have available. In other words, calm your initial feelings of aggression or fear, and investigate with an open mind and Social Intelligence the person before you.

This will give you *Insight;* will allow you to make far-more appropriate responses to the individual you are meeting; and will rapidly increase the probability of a mutually successful social interaction.

Stereotypes lurk like monsters in our brains, and even something as 'simple' as a person's name can unconsciously colour our perceptions of that person.

Luke Birmingham, a forensic psychiatrist at the University of Southampton, in an elegant little experiment, demonstrated how your name can affect the way people judge you ...

Birmingham asked 464 British psychiatrists to provide a diagnosis based on a 'one-page description' of a 24-year-old man who had assaulted a train conductor.

When the psychiatrists were asked to assess 'Matthew', over three-quarters gave him a sympathetic hearing, suggesting that the poor young man was in need of medical help, and was probably suffering from schizophrenia.

When the same young man was presented as 'Wayne', the psychiatrists gave him a much-more sinister character evaluation. 'Wayne' was *twice* as likely as 'Matthew' to be diagnosed as a malingerer, a drug abuser, and to be suffering from a personality disorder!

Even more alarming – studies show that negative social stereotypes can affect the way that we judge *ourselves* and our abilities.

Case Study – Told I Can't: Think I Can't

Paul Davis, of the University of Waterloo in Ontario, set out to examine the impact of stereotype-loaded advertising on young women studying mathematics at the University. He had selected them because they all described themselves as being good at maths and that they considered the skill important to them.

To his surprise, Davis found that simply watching two sexist television commercials undermining the ability of the female brain, significantly diminished the ability of the young women to solve difficult maths problems immediately after having viewed the commercials.

In the second part of this experiment, Davis showed the advertisements to female undergraduates before they made their subject choices at the University. Those who saw the negative stereotyping significantly shifted the subject they said they would like to specialize in away from mathematics and the sciences.

The same advertisements also caused these highly motivated young women to avoid taking the leadership role in a two-person task.

There is strong evidence to suggest that when you 'put a person down' in this manner, not only do you restrict their mental choices and freedom: you direct their life and its future in a negative and diminishing way. This is not a recommended way of increasing the Social Intelligence of yourself, other people or the planet as a whole!

In addition to this negative social effect, such demeaning statements also have a negative effect on the other individuals' immune systems, generally weakening their defences against stress-related and other diseases.

In one experiment, elderly people were subjected to 10 minutes of stereotype-triggering words to do with ageing – one group being shown positive words, and the other negative ones. They were then given a series of mathematical problems to solve.

Those shown the negative words became very stressed when presented with the problems. Their heart rates, blood pressure and skin conductivity all increased significantly, and stayed at an unnaturally high level for more than 30 minutes.

In stark contrast, those bolstered by positive cues sailed through the challenge with no signs of stress at all.

Moreover, negative stereotyping of *any* group, even if it is one to which you do not belong, negatively affects *you* personally.

John Bargh, a Social Psychologist at New York State University, set out to see if negative age stereotypes would in anyway take their toll on college students. One group of students had to unscramble sentences scattered with neutral words relating to age. The second group had an identical task, except that their sentences were scattered with age-related words that were particularly negative.

The amazing result? The students who had dealt with the negative words remembered significantly less about the experiment than the students who had sorted neutral words. Perhaps even more significantly, students who had dealt with the negative words 'became suddenly older'. Unknown to them, their behaviour as they

> left the room was being monitored. They moved significantly more
> slowly as they walked away, and, even though in the prime of youth,
> were in physical appearance and movement much closer to the
> negative word descriptions of old age than were the neutral group.

positive attitoods

From his experiments, reported above, John Bargh concluded that the images stored in our minds have extraordinary power over our behaviours. *But those images don't have to be negative: they can be positive ones too.* And positive images can be just as powerful, if not more so, than negative images, as this next story shows.

Brad Humphrey and the No-Hope Teenagers

Brad Humphrey, a teacher and social worker in San Diego, focused his work on those teenagers from the ghetto on whom everyone else had given up – street kids, drug dealers, those in psychiatric units or jail. Their average life expectancy was a mere 20 years.

Brad's goal was to transform the teenagers' horribly negative attitudes about themselves and to completely remake their self-images. He did this by providing them with brain and body training. In the beginning, for example, he tested their memories and found them unusually poor. He then focused on the worst child in the class, a young girl, and took her aside while he sent the others on a half-an-hour run.

While they were running Brad quickly trained the young girl in memory techniques, teaching her how she could easily remember a list of 20 objects perfectly. When the others came back, he challenged them to give the young girl 20 random objects for her to memorize. Scoffingly they did so, knowing that she had a terrible memory and assuming that she would mess the whole thing up. Imagine their surprise (and their change of attitude!) when she rattled the 20 off perfectly: forwards and backwards.

The experience changed the attitude of the others towards the girl, and more especially *changed the girl's attitude towards herself and her own abilities.*

For two solid years Brad taught the group physical and mental strengthening techniques. At the end of the two-year period, the teenagers had been transformed from no-hope, self-destructive down-and-outs into fit, confident young adults, determined to transform other teenagers' negative, depressing and life-threatening attitudes.

The climax of the two years came when Brad introduced the teenagers to a 500-strong audience of senior educators, university professors, head teachers and writers at an educational conference in Bellingham, Washington. The 17 teenagers, all radiantly fit and self-assured, proceeded to take on the audience in all forms of mental combat, including memory games, creative thinking and other mind sports.

The teenagers thrashed the educators!

Brad Humphrey's work confirmed, beyond any reasonable doubt, that with the right care and love, attitudes can be changed; and when attitudes change, lives change.

self-confidence – what everyone should know

Brad succeeded because he believed in the children, and believed that he could reawaken their self-confidence and self-belief.

Self-confidence is the key to Social Intelligence and success. If you have belief in yourself and your own strengths and abilities, you will find it much easier to relax and 'be yourself' in any social situation. This, in turn, will allow others to relax and enjoy your company.

This principle is probably one of the most important that we can instil in our children. A self-confident child, secure in the knowledge of his or her own worth, will not have to go around 'proving' anything to the other kids in the playground – literally throwing his or her weight around.

Self-confident children (just like Brad's teenagers) will have the self-respect, the motivation and determination to go out and achieve their own personal goals in life. They will have a 'life vision' (see Chapter 4).

Unfortunately, insecure, unsure children often try to undermine other children to prove just how 'big' and 'important' they are, either in their own eyes, or in the eyes of 'their gang'.

In just the same way, unconfident and insecure adults try to prove their worth by, for example, dominating their workmates or by being an unreasonable and bullying boss. Being on the receiving end of such behaviour will often undermine the victim's sense of self-worth and esteem – precisely as it is intended to do.

This is why it is so vital that we give our children (and ourselves!) the Socially Intelligent skill of positive self-confidence.

Negative thoughts produce negative attitudes; positive thoughts produce positive attitudes. And the more often those thoughts are repeated, the stronger those attitudes become.

Spotlight on Prejudice

Alan Hart, a Social Psychologist at Amherst College in Massachusetts, used magnetic resonance imaging to track deep-rooted prejudice. He showed people images of black and white faces, and checked the reactions of the *amygdala* – a part of the brain that is thought to act like a spotlight, focusing attention of fearful or other emotionally charged events.

Faces of a different colour to the subject's consistently triggered more *amygdala* activity.

This is why repeating positive affirmations or sayings is so powerful when it comes to changing our behaviour.

Studies of brain cells confirm that once you have the thought, be it positive or negative, the probability of having that thought again is increased. Repetition of any thought increases the repetition of that thought. If we wish to have happier, more successful, confident lives, we need to make increasingly sure that our thoughts are positively directed towards others. This will increase the probability that they will feel positive towards us, and the positive cycle of happier and more productive social relationships has begun.

'There is nothing either good or bad, but thinking makes it so.'

(Shakespeare)

Now that you have a good grasp of the way in which attitude towards sex, age, race and indeed any other characteristic of any other individual can positively or negatively affect both them and yourself, you are ready for a workout that will accentuate the positive. This will benefit others, you, and especially your Social Intelligence.

social workout

Prejudice Audit

Do a personal audit of your own possible prejudices. Do a mini-Mind Map® (see Chapter 3) on your traditional thoughts about the main characteristics of the following groups:

- Males
- Females
- Children
- The elderly
- Academics
- Sports men and women
- Politicians
- Different racial groups

Check your responses for any negative stereotypes, and investigate the reasons why these negative ideas arose. Compare them with any positive thoughts you had, and see if you can spot any pattern between the two. For example, if you know many members of a particular group (footballers for instance), you will probably have fewer negative ideas about them than a group you have had less dealings with (politicians, for example), because you know the latter group less well. You should find this exploration entertaining, invigorating and enlightening.

Think through these issues, and if necessary, open your mind to wider experiences. This will strengthen the power of your Social Intelligence, and also broaden your social sphere.

Monitor Your Conversations

When you are with family, colleagues and friends, notice the way in which you consciously or unconsciously support or criticize them.

Knowing as you now do that negative expectations/criticism actually helps them to become worse, and that positive expectations and words of support significantly contribute to their success, adjust your social conversations to a more positive and supportive style.

Monitor Your Internal Conversations

The same thing applies to the conversations that you hold with yourself.

Praise yourself, be supportive of your efforts, and celebrate your own achievements – especially when they are those little, personal achievements that others do not, or cannot notice.

social brain boosters

- I am increasingly developing my 'Flight! Fight! Insight' response.
- People from other nations, with different customs and of different races are of increasing fascination to me.
- My self-confidence is growing more and more.
- My attitudes are increasingly positive.

In the next chapter you will discover how your own positive attitudes and prejudice will be a huge boon to successful negotiations.

negotiations –

how to win friends and influence people

chapter seven

'If someone disagrees with me, my job is to change his mind? No! If someone disagrees with me, my job is to let him do so.'

(Andrew Matthews)

It is the natural goal of every human to win friends, to influence people, to be popular, to come out of negotiations successfully, and to deal with social relationships in a way that produces the results they desire.

Negotiation is an amazingly important Social Intelligence skill to perfect. Most people will associate the word 'negotiation' with business and the world of work, but it is just as important in our everyday, domestic lives.

The goal of any negotiations is to end up with agreement between all sides involved, so that everyone goes away happy with the outcome. This applies just as much to deals stuck between parents and teenagers on how late youngsters can stay out at a party, as to negotiations about pay and working conditions between unions and management. The Social Intelligence involved is the same.

First, here is an incredible story of negotiation and cooperation from the animal world.

an amazing animal story

A Canadian Natural History film crew set out to film something that had never been filmed before – a year in the life of a pack of wolves, following them with helicopters so that they could film aerial views of the wolves' annual migration with their main source of food, the reindeer.

The first great surprise concerning animal social behaviour came when the crew observed the relationship between the reindeer herd and the wolf pack.

It had been assumed by everyone that on its migration, the reindeer herd kept to itself, with the wolf pack following behind. Again it was assumed that the wolf pack made regular 'sneak attacks' on the reindeer, 'cowardly' attacking only the most frail and feeble.

However, the truth was astonishing: the reindeer herd and wolf pack travelled *together!* Not only did they travel together, they were actually *friends!* For days on end they would run together, play together and rest together.

Only when the wolves became hungry did the relationships change, and even this was a mutually understood arrangement. The leader of the wolf pack, a massive 'she-wolf', would suddenly 'freeze', signalling to her main hunters that the chase was on. The reindeer would calmly gather into a closer, more densely packed bunch, and wait for the wolves' 'go' signal. As soon as this was given, everything proceeded in a socially agreed pattern. The wolves chose only one reindeer as their target. This was sometimes a weaker one, although sometimes a more normal member of the herd.

The chase lasted usually for a maximum of 10 minutes, and most of the time the wolves were successful. Once the target had been selected, the remainder of the deer relaxed and carried on life as usual.

The wolves were not always successful. In about one case out of five, the strong and resilient deer would escape back into the herd. Did the wolves keep chasing or pick another less-resilient deer? No! They accepted the 'deal' and agreed to go hungry for a day or two more. Until the wolves were ready to eat again, the herd and the pack lived together once more as travelling companions, the wolves protecting the herd from other predators, and the herd providing the occasional sustenance for the wolves.

All of this was amazing, but more amazing was yet to come!

One day the lead helicopter of the filming crew reported that the wolf pack was heading in the general direction of the carcass of a massive moose. What especially excited the pilot was that two other beasts had scented the carcass, and were simultaneously heading towards it from different directions. The first was a giant grizzly bear, the second a wolverine. The wolverine is an animal somewhat like a cross between a badger and a racoon. Although it is relatively small, it is commonly known as one of the best pound-for-pound fighters in the world. With its claws and teeth it can easily break into the toughest mountain lodge, and with one bite of its teeth can snap in two a can of tinned food.

The she-wolf had already detached herself from the pack to investigate the tantalizing scent, and the helicopter pilot was enthusiastically anticipating the greatest animal punch-up ever filmed.

What do you think happened?

What the film showed was extraordinary and completely unpredicted. The three lethal fighters arrived at the clearing at roughly the same time, each having already become aware of the others' presence. But, rather than posturing aggressively and immediately getting into a free-for-all, they each calmly surveyed the others and sat down in the snow. They waited, and watched ...

The she-wolf, in the manner of a cat stalking a bird, very gently moved one paw forward, paused, checked with the other two animals, and having been given the signal that everything was so far okay, moved another paw forward. This process she repeated, agonizingly slowly, until she had arrived at the carcass.

There, still checking with the others that everything was okay, she incredibly gently, and with an obviously studied purpose of making no rapid movements, took a large bite out of the carcass, and with the same cautious, cat-like movement with which she had approached it, returned to her original spot.

As soon as she had retreated to her original spot, the bear *did exactly the same thing! And then so did the wolverine!*

The three animals repeated the same procedure time and time again, each taking its turn, each constantly checking with the others, and each taking only its own 'fair share' with each turn.

It was a perfect, slow-motion winter social ballet!

And why had the three toughest, meanest and best fighters in the animal kingdom given up the opportunity for the ultimate slug-fest and accolade as 'the greatest fighter of all time'? Because, unlike those who were willing them on to such a combat, they were more Socially Intelligent! Each one of them, through experience and an exquisite ability to read body language, was aware of both the needs and power of the others. Each was aware that it did have the strength and fighting skills to win in combat. Each was also aware that in such combat, even if it should win, there would be an almost 100 per cent certainty of sustaining some serious injury that would be both an immediate and a long-term threat to its survival.

They thus all made the most intelligent decision: to consider each other's needs; to share a resource which provided for all three of them; to conserve their energy; and to preserve themselves intact rather than risk serious wounds.

When each was satisfied, you could almost sense them giving a 'nod and a wink' to the others, after which they calmly turned and returned to the wilderness by the path on which they had arrived.

The helicopter pilot, having seen something far greater than he had expected, was reduced to an awed silence.

'win-win' solutions

In negotiation-speak, the animals in the story above had all opted for the 'win-win' solution, where everyone comes away feeling satisfied with the outcome.

True negotiation takes place when each side respects the other, and their point of view, and enters into the discussion positively. If you are determined that your solution, and your particular solution *only*, is the correct one – to be imposed on the other side if necessary – that is not negotiation; it is dictatorship.

If you have enough power or influence in this instance, you will be able to impose your solution, but you can be sure that the other side will not be happy with it, and will possibly do all that they can to frustrate your plans in the future. Storing up resentment is not a Socially Intelligent thing to do!

'the way of harmony' vs. the way of the world

The difference between Socially Intelligent negotiation, and the (unfortunately) all-too-common approach of many people to resolving disagreements and conflicts, is epitomized by the differences between the martial arts of karate and Aikido.

In karate, if someone is throwing a punch at your face, you endeavour to block it with your fist, hopefully damaging your opponent's wrist in the process, and swinging his arm off target. As it veers away, exposing your opponent's ribcage, your goal is to punch into that ribcage. Your opponent, however, as he is being shoved off balance, is trained to find unguarded areas of your abdomen, groin or legs, and to attack them in the process of going off balance. Your task, of course, is to block any such attack and, with your elbow, to strike down on the falling body.

And so the process continues until one of you is a bloody heap on the ground, and the other victorious (and probably damaged!). (Does this remind you of the bear, the wolf, the wolverine and the helicopter pilot?!)

The founder of Aikido ('the way of harmony'), Morihei Ueshiba, was one of Japan's top karate practitioners. He observed that over the years, despite his regular victories, he was becoming increasingly damaged. It struck him that this was not the way to spend the rest of his life! He determined to find a more profound, harmonious, socially and spiritually congruent form of physical art.

In the sport he developed, Aikido, if someone attempts to punch you in the face, you do not need to block the punch. It is much more efficient and harmonious to move ever so slightly (that's all you need to do!) to the side, to allow the punch to pass by harmlessly, and to help direct it on its way with your own balance and firm guidance.

Aikido means 'way of harmony', and it is based on reading the other person's mind and body-language, and using that person's energy to your advantage, even if they are attacking you. Aikido allows you to maintain your own position, to relate to others and simultaneously to 'go with the flow'.

Every time someone tries to strike you in any way, you simply move slightly aside, move towards your opponent's centre and 'see the world' from his perspective. If you are balanced and your opponent not, the probability of damage to either of you is minimal, especially if you are of peaceful intent.

There is a wonderful story that encapsulates all these points, told by the authors of *Body Learning* (Michael Gelb) and *Emotional Intelligence* (Daniel Goleman), which concerns the late Terry Dobson, who in the 1950s was one of the first Westerners ever to study this superb martial art in Japan.

Terry's Story

One afternoon I was riding home on a suburban Tokyo train when a huge, bellicose and very drunk labourer got on. The man began terrorizing the passengers: screaming curses, he took a swing at a woman holding a baby, sending her sprawling in the laps of an elderly couple, who then jumped up and joined a stampede to the other end of the carriage. The drunk, taking a few more random swings, grabbed the metal pole in the middle of the carriage with a roar and tried to tear it out of its socket.

At that point I felt called upon to intervene, lest someone get seriously hurt. But I recalled the words of my teacher:

'Aikido is the art of reconciliation. Whoever has the mind to fight has broken his connection with the universe. If you try to dominate people; you are already defeated. We study how to resolve conflict, not how to start it.'

Indeed, I had agreed, upon beginning lessons with my teacher, never to pick a fight, and to use my martial-arts skills only in self-defence. Now, at last, I saw my chance to test my Aikido abilities in real life, in what was clearly a legitimate opportunity. So, as all the other passengers sat frozen in their seats, I stood up, slowly and with deliberation.

Seeing me, the drunk roared, 'Aha! A foreigner! You need a lesson in Japanese manners!' and began gathering himself to take me on.

But just as the drunk was on the verge of making his move, someone gave an ear-splitting, oddly joyous shout: 'Hey!'

The shout had the cheery tone of someone who has suddenly come upon a fond friend. The drunk, surprised, spun around to see a tiny Japanese man sitting there, probably in his seventies. The old man beamed with delight at the drunk, and beckoned him over with a light wave of his hand and a lilting 'C'mere'.

The drunk strode over with a belligerent, 'Why the hell should I talk to you?' Meanwhile, I was ready to fell the drunk in a moment if he made the least violent move.

'What'cha been drinking?' the old man asked, his eyes beaming at the drunken labourer.

'I been drinking sake, and it's none of your business,' the drunk bellowed.

'Oh, that's wonderful, absolutely wonderful,' the old man replied in a warm tone. 'You see I love sake, too. Every night, me and my wife (she's seventy-six, you know), we warm up a little bottle of sake and take it out into the garden, and we sit on an old wooden bench ...' He continued on about the persimmon tree in his backyard, the fortunes of his garden, enjoying sake in the evening.

The drunk's face began to soften as he listened to the old man; his fists unclenched. 'Yeah ... I love persimmons, too ... ,' he said, his voice trailing off.

'Yes,' the old man replied in a sprightly voice, 'and I'm sure you have a wonderful wife.'

'No,' said the labourer. 'My wife died ...' Sobbing, he launched into a sad tale of losing his wife, his home, his job, of being ashamed of himself.

Just then the train came to my stop, and as I was getting off I turned to hear the old man invite the drunk to join him and tell him all about it, and to see the drunk sprawl along the seat, his head in the old man's lap.

This remarkable story exhibits the fundamental social truth that the best way to win friends, influence people, negotiate and resolve conflicts is to remain personally strong, while completely understanding and entering the other person's domain.

Aikido and its principles are precisely what the old man in the story was practising.

Coming back to our own social relationships, negotiations, influence and attempts at resolving conflicts, our traditional approach in such situations has been far more the karate approach. We go powering in, attacking left, right and centre, trying to prove our point, argue our case, win the debate, change that friend and dominate the interaction. This inevitably creates resistance, and the fight is on – often to the total disadvantage of both the personal relationships and the mutual goals!

The 'way-of-harmony' approach is much more successful, much more powerful, far less damaging and much more enjoyable than other approaches.

negotiating the aikido way!

Whenever you are in any sort of negotiations, whether at work or at home, try using the following negotiating principles to reach an outcome acceptable to all the parties:

- Before starting make sure that you know *precisely* what it is you want, and the *maximum price* you would be willing to pay - whether that price is in money, time, emotions, or anything else.

For example: you want your son to complete an important school assignment by the end of the week *(goal)*; if he stays in and does the work, you promise that you will take him fishing with you at the weekend *(price)*.

- Enter the negotiations in a positive, friendly frame of mind.

If you are feeling uptight and defensive, you are unlikely to reach any sort of solution with which you feel happy.

- Have your facts at your fingertips. Nothing makes you so vulnerable in negotiations as ignorance!

If you ask your boss for a pay rise, because you think that your job responsibilities have expanded way beyond your original duties, make sure that you have solid evidence to back your claim when you go in to negotiate – reports or projects you have worked on. Mind Map® the points you want to raise to prepare yourself beforehand.

- Find out the goals of your opposite number.

Ask them what they want from the meeting first, before you even attempt to put your own wishes across. You will often find that there are many more common bonds than you had anticipated, and that also many of the obstacles and barriers you were expecting do not, in fact, exist.

- Time. You have lots of it! One of the best ways to disadvantage yourself in negotiations is to appear rushed or hurried. Those with whom you are negotiating may well have a deadline, and if they know that you are not in a hurry they will become more anxious to complete as time goes on, leaving you in the advantageous position.

There is the wonderful story concerning the delicate negotiations that went on between the USA and the Soviet Union to reduce the numbers of nuclear warheads each side had. At the beginning of one session (held in a neutral third country), the Americans, reckoning on their being there for some time, booked themselves into the most comfortable hotel in town. The Soviets, unable to afford such luxurious accommodation, nevertheless went one better – the negotiators' wives and partners arrived on the next flight to keep them company for as long as the talks lasted!

■ Be sensitive to the other person's body language.

As we saw in Chapter 2, the ability to read the subtle (and not-so-subtle) signals people make unconsciously is an invaluable Social Intelligence skill in negotiations.

■ Win-Win. Always negotiate from a win-win standpoint. If you do this those with whom you are negotiating will know that you are, in a real sense, on their side. This will make them much warmer and more open to you, will encourage them to 'negotiate for you', and the ideal situation of everybody negotiating for everybody else's benefit will be achieved.

Success!

Your Social Workout will give you some practise!

social workout

Look for the Positive

Look for the good in your friends, colleagues and fellow negotiators. This is especially important when you are in disagreement with someone. Make sure that you remember the 'way of harmony' and try not to reduce your negotiations to a slanging match!

Respect the person as a unique individual. Everyone (including you) loves to be recognized for their finer qualities and their accomplishments. And everyone (also including you) has such finer qualities!

The reverse of this is to cut to an absolute minimum any tendency to criticize, condemn or complain.

Where Possible, Avoid Argument

This does not mean you have to avoid meaty or weighty discussions in which you strongly voice your opinion. But it does mean avoiding those situations in which each one of you is trying to prove that your perspective is the *only* one that is correct, while the perspective of the others is, by definition, wrong.

Take the Aikido path!

See the Other Person's Point of View

Empathize and sympathize with the other person's ideas, desires and goals. This principle may seem hard to follow, especially if you are personally directly opposed to everything they stand for! It is however, easier than you think. Remember, you are in the process of building relationships, *not* scoring debating points. In these situations consider yourself more like an investigative reporter who is simply trying to find out everything about the interviewee.

If you take this approach you will become a master at seeing things from the other person's point of view, one of the true signs of genius on the Social Intelligence scale!

Own Up to Your Mistakes

There are few things more annoying than a person who refuses to admit that he or she has made a mistake, and who continues to waste valuable social time defending an untenable position!

Refusing to admit mistakes shows you to be arrogant, lacking in basic self-confidence, and, in a deep sense, dishonest with both yourself and others.

When you admit mistakes, do it immediately, emphatically and enthusiastically! This will show that you are honest with yourself and others, open, flexible, wanting to learn and non-aggressive: one who will probably give good feedback and advice and be reliable as a supportive friend.

What better colleague or friend could you want?!

social brain boosters

- ■ I am practising Aikido in my personal relationships.
- ■ I am an increasingly competent negotiator.
- ■ I go for the win-win in all social situations.

In the next chapter we look at how to apply your Social Intelligence to boost your Social Graces!

social graces –

or what to do when...

chapter eight

'Manners maketh man'

(traditional proverb)

A great deal has been written on the subject of 'manners', with books on 'social etiquette' laying down in minute detail exactly what to do and how to behave 'properly' at specific social occasions. Don't worry – I'm not going to do that here!

Instead I will look at some of the reasons why 'good manners' can be seen as an integral part of Social Intelligence, and how you can use them to keep and increase your friends and acquaintances.

showing appreciation

Everyone likes to be appreciated, and Socially Intelligent people will make sure that they show appreciation of people, thanking them for favours, for doing their job well, or simply for being there.

You can, however, maximize the impact of your thanks and appreciation by thinking about and applying what you have already learned in *The Power of Social Intelligence*.

Saying Thanks

When you wish to express appreciation to people, remember that *they* will remember it better if you do so near the end of your time together. Make sure that you are both relaxed and alert when you give your thanks, in order to increase the energy and meaning with which you give it. You will thus ensure that its impact both in intensity and timing will be maximized.

To reinforce your 'thank you', send a letter or note of thanks the next day too – and not just after social events at someone's house. A short note saying something like 'Thanks for meeting me yesterday, it was good to be able to discuss ...', or 'Thank you for interviewing me for the vacancy ...' will ensure that you are remembered very positively after the event, and will give you a thoughtful and considerate reputation.

Another way to ensure that your thanks has extra meaning for the receiver, is to say *why* you are saying thank you: 'thank you for your patience/your advice' to a shop assistant who has been helping you make up your mind about which pair of shoes to buy; 'thank you for your skill' to the electrician who fixes your cooker; 'thanks for the smooth drive' to a taxi driver, and so on.

If you say why you are thanking someone, you are sure to be rewarded with a big smile, and 'you're welcome!' in return.

You can take this one stage further. If you've received outstanding service from someone, don't just thank them – thank their boss, or write to the organization they represent and say that you've been impressed by their efficiency and professionalism. (This tends to be especially appreciated where the organization is more used to receiving complaints rather than praise!)

Giving Gifts

Giving gifts is another way of showing your appreciation to someone. Most people will take a bottle of wine to a party or dinner they have been invited to, but often these simply end up plonked down with other contributions in the general melee at the start of the event. If you want your gift to be remembered (and by extension, *you* to be remembered), try to make it outstanding and different – an unusual potted plant, for example, or a small ornament. Such a gift does not have to be very large or expensive, but just something which shows that you have thought about your host and what they would like.

You don't need a special reason to give someone some small gift, or a greetings card. Spotting something in a shop, or coming across some attractive shells or unusual pebbles on a beach and thinking that a particular person would like them, shows you to be a thoughtful, caring friend.

celebrating in style

Celebrations such as birthdays, anniversaries and special holidays mark significant events, and it is important that we mark them with rituals and ceremonies that further imprint the event on our memories.

Birthdays and anniversaries are what? Von Restorffs! We celebrate them to remind ourselves of their importance, to re-celebrate the fact that they were once 'firsts' and to remind our family and friends that we do consider these to be special days for them. By remembering the events, we remember and celebrate the people involved.

This is particularly important if we don't see the people very often. Sending a card or a gift to your brother and sister-in-law at the other end of the country on their wedding anniversary demonstrates that you think of the event, and them, as important enough to mark the occasion in some special way.

other people's customs

It is very important to be aware of the customs of other cultures, and to be sensitive to the feelings of others. This is especially true in business. It is more and more important to be aware of different ways of doing things the more international business becomes. But it is equally important when on holiday visits to other countries and cultures.

Offering a teetotal Muslim a bottle of wine may not be seen as the friendly gesture that you intend, and while it is regarded as polite to use your left hand while eating in the UK, for example, in some Arab countries it is regarded as very rude.

An example of how different cultures have very differing customs and cultures can be seen in the way that something as ordinary as a business card is treated in Japan and other Asian countries, compared to the way it is handled in the West.

Greetings Rituals – The Asian Way

The most common global modern method of ritual greeting is the handing over of a business card.

The current masters of this art are the Asian countries. So let us examine in detail their ritual, find the reasons behind it, and extract valuable lessons from it. The step-by-step procedure is as follows:

1. You hand your card, face up, with the print legible to the person to whom you are handing it. You offer it with *both* hands.
2. You simultaneously receive the other person's card.

Reasons:
- By handing the card with two hands you each have to be facing each other and to be relatively close to each other. Contact and relative intimacy is already being established.
- Holding the print so that it is legible is a simple act of consideration.

- Exchanging cards simultaneously confirms the equality of the relationship from the outset, and the mutual respect for each other.

3. Having received the card, you each spend a moment reading it thoroughly and examining its quality.
4. You comment on some positive aspects of the card's content/quality.

Reasons:
- The pause to consider the card means that you are receiving the other person's offering with openness and interest, and indicating that this is of paramount importance to you.
- Commenting on the card confirms that you have absorbed its contents and considered their meaning.
- Looking for the positive establishes that you are interested in a productive, co-operative and positive relationship.

5. Unless you are leaving immediately, you do *not* put the card in your pocket straightaway. You place it on a surface where it remains constantly visible throughout your time with each other.

Reasons:
- Immediately stuffing the card in your pocket is a sign of disrespect, symbolically indicating that you have finished with that person's identity.

---

social graces – or what to do when ...

- Placing it on a surface where it is visible symbolizes the fact that you regard that individual and the individual's identity as important factors in the environment.
- Having the card constantly in front of you makes reference to it easy, and the repetition of its contents in your brain guarantees that you will have a better chance of remembering both the name and the associations surrounding it.

Greetings Rituals – The Western Way

Consider by comparison the common Western ritual, in which the card is given with one hand, neither looked at nor commented upon, and immediately stuffed somewhere where it is out of sight – and out of mind!

Greetings rituals, well used, can make meeting and remembering new people easier and more enjoyable; it can make our friends, family and colleagues feel remembered, appreciated and loved; it can give us a wonderful sense of anticipation; can act as von Restorff markers throughout our years and lives.

sharing the bad times

A social obligation that many people find very hard is to offer comfort and condolences to people who have been bereaved or who have just received some piece of terrible news.

We know that we should say something, but have no idea what words to use that do not sound trite and insincere. Because we are scared of 'getting it wrong', and embarrassed imagining how the person will react, often we end up doing or saying nothing.

Sitting down and writing a short note saying that you are thinking of the person and their family is a difficult task, but it will be greatly appreciated by the recipient. As always, it's not so much the words themselves that are important, but the care and thought behind them. Just knowing that people are thinking of you at such a hard time is a great comfort for many.

Alternatively, you could send flowers, which again shows that you are thinking of the person. If you live nearby, maybe you could offer more practical help – picking the children up from school, taking round a ready-cooked meal – just something to help out. Or there is the simple, sympathetic hug, to show that the person is not alone (which is what many people feel at moments of crisis).

social workout

Plan Positive Rituals

At the beginning of your year, when you are planning your diary, look ahead to all those possible celebrations and ceremonies in which you would like to be involved. Consider the birthdays, anniversaries and other special dates you would like to mark. Put them in your diary in some coloured and picture form in order to make them more appealing, and begin to plan how you are going to make the most of them for yourself and your friends. Think of special things you can do to make those occasions more enjoyable for those with whom you will be.

Cultural Differences

Begin to study differences in the rituals and ceremonies of different cultures. In some, for example, death is mourned; in others it is celebrated. For some death is symbolized in ritual ceremonies by white, in others by black. In some cultures, encircling the thumb and forefinger is a symbol of 'A Okay'; in others it is an extremely obscene gesture!

Make a study of cultural social differences a hobby – you will reap wonderful rewards (and may also save yourself some considerable embarrassment and hassle!).

social brain boosters

- I increasingly realize that saying 'thank you' is one of the greatest rewards I can give to others.

- I increasingly use positive rituals to make the lives of my friends happier and more fulfilled.

In the next chapter I will show you how you can engage your whole brain on your road to social success, and will give you a wonderful example of a Social Intelligence Star.

chapter nine

'The expression one wears on one's face is far more important than the clothes one wears on one's back.'

(Dale Carnegie)

If you apply everything you have so far learned in *The Power of Social Intelligence*, you will automatically be a successful social operator. In this chapter we are going to start with the fascinating study that sets the scene by giving some new insights into the nature of social relations.

I will also recap the major Social Intelligence characteristics, and provide a wonderful example of a 'Social Intelligence Star'. Finally there is a Social Intelligence questionnaire, for you to gauge just how far you have expanded and developed your Social IQ.

Case Study – The Death of a Nasty Assumption!

For centuries researchers and the public have agreed on the rather unpleasant 'truth' that the only reason we humans tend to co-operate is self interest.

Now, happily, a much more complex, sophisticated and positive picture is emerging from recent studies.

Anthropologist Joseph Henrich of the University of Michigan, and his colleague Robert Boyd of the University of California in Los Angeles, studied the transmission of social behaviour and culture among humans. They came to a startling conclusion: co-operation is *not* the result of selfishness: it is the result of two major 'Brain Tendencies'. According to Henrich:

'There are two elements of human psychology that we know about: one is that *people have a tendency to copy the majority*; the other is that *people have a tendency to copy the most successful individual*.

'What we are able to show is that because humans rely on copying the successful and the majority, this creates a stable co-operative equilibrium which doesn't exist if those two cultural mechanisms aren't in place.'

This 'double mimicking' leads to a positive spiral of success. Co-operation leads to a high probability of more food, better health, more creativity, more general energy and therefore more powerful economic growth for the community as a whole.

This spiralling success will be seen by outsiders, who themselves will want to copy the successful group and the successful individuals within that group. When enough individuals from other groups start mimicking those of the successful group, the groups which are not so Socially Intelligent become more so, and begin to reap the same benefits as the originally successful Socially Intelligent group.

Henrich further points out that we are probably the most sociable of all living creatures. 'Humans co-operate in larger groups. When humans go to war, for example, they will co-operate with large numbers of individuals they are unrelated to and probably won't see again.'

And if you think about it, one of the social achievements that may separate us from all other living creatures, is the queue! Without the co-operation of total strangers a queue would quickly break down and chaos result!

whole-brain thinking

Many of us, unwittingly, make ourselves half-witted (or less!) in social situations, by only using *half* of our social and intellectual brain skills! You have probably heard of the 'Left Brain/Right Brain' model, which shows that we have two main sets of intellectual/social skills, divided between the right and left hemispheres of our brains:

Left Brain	Right Brain
Words	Rhythm
Logic	Spatial awareness
Numbers	Imagination
Sequence	Daydreaming
Analysis	Colour
Lists	Holistic (gestalt) awareness

Because of a century's-long emphasis on the 'Left Brain', analytical skills, we have tended to dominate our social interactions with words, logic, numbers, analysis and linearity.

We have done this at the expense of our 'Right Brain', intuitive skills. (This was partly the trap I fell into in the early development of my Social Intelligence, see page 6.)

Just imagine spending an entire evening with a group of people who used *only* their left-brain skills! What single word would sum up such an evening?

BORING!

Next imagine an evening with a group of friends who used only their right-brain skills. You would probably have a lot of fun – but it would have been chaos! Conversation would have been almost non-existent; the music would have had no order, sequence, pattern or structure; and the venue would be a wreck!

By using only half their mental skills, your imaginary friends would actually have been using *less than half* their full complement of skills, because the left and right brain skills are best used together, where they create a multiplying, synergistic effect, and bring out the best of both brains!

Socially successful people will use *all* of their phenomenal brainpower when interacting with other people, and will use imagination and planning, for example, simultaneously to show concern for others, and to amuse and delight their friends and companions.

Make sure that you use all your whole-brain skills. In this way you will appeal to the 'whole brain' of your companions.

the characteristics of social intelligence

So what are the necessary qualities and characteristics of Social Intelligence?

1. The confidence to be yourself
2. A life vision – to know where you're going
3. An abiding interest in other people
4. Respect for others
5. Empathy, and the ability to read and use body language to do this
6. Awareness of when it is appropriate to speak, and when to listen
7. A positive attitude

All these characteristics are epitomized by our Social Intelligence Star – Oprah Winfrey.

Oprah Winfrey – Social Intelligence Star

Oprah Winfrey, businesswoman, award-winning actress, and the host of the top-rated US talk show, is probably one of the best-known and influential women in the world. Tens of millions in over 130 countries watch her daily TV show, which is unique for its social 'rapport' format.

Oprah's phenomenal success is due to her instinctive empathy with her audience, her personal honesty, and her positive attitude in the face of adversity. The conversational style of show allows and encourages the sharing of feelings, emotions and experiences. As one participant has put it, Oprah 'makes people care *because she cares*'.

Instead of a Social Workout for this chapter, I have included a Social Intelligence Questionnaire. It is designed to help you think about what you have learned reading through *The Power of Social Intelligence*, and to give you further 'food for thought'!

social intelligence survey questionnaire

Check each of the following questions 'True' or 'False' – 'True' if the statement generally or absolutely applies to you; 'False' if it generally or absolutely does not. Use your answers as guides and beacons for your own Social Intelligence goals in your life.

1. I love people and the human-race in general   True/False

2. I believe standard IQ is more important than Social Intelligence as a measure of succes   True/False

3. I believe standard IQ is more important than Social Intelligence as a measure of happiness   True/False

4. I consider first meetings of extreme importance   True/False

5. I consider 'farewells' and partings of extreme importance   True/False

6. The use of imagination is not especially important in social relationships   True/False

7. Being fixated on a life vision tends to destroy social relationships   True/False

8. Sensual people form weak bonds with others   True/False

9. Copying is a sign of weakness and should be avoided True/False

10. Creativity is for 'wimps'   True/False

11. The body is at least as important a conveyor of communication as spoken words   True/False

12. There are many bodily expressions that are common to all human cultures and societies   True/False

13. Smiling at people usually makes them either shy or aggressive True/False

14. Positive people are generally disregarded by others as too 'airy fairy'   True/False

15. In social situations, 'honesty is the best policy'   True/False

16. People do tend to 'live up' or 'down' to the expectations of others True/False

17. Nearly everybody at some time needs time alone, 'space' to be with themselves   True/False

---

18. Being able to prove that someone is wrong, is a good way to win an argument   True/False

19. 'Winning' a conflict requires greater power   True/False

20. Most speakers are naturally boring   True/False

21. My first impressions of people are usually not accurate   True/False

22. I enjoy entertaining friends for parties, dinners and social functions   True/False

23. I am persuasive in negotiations   True/False

24. I usually let other people resolve conflicts   True/False

25. I have always had a good rapport with people   True/False

26. I am extremely sensitive to the moods of others   True/False

27. I am good at remembering people's faces   True/False

28. I am good at remembering people's names   True/False

29. It doesn't really matter what other people think of me
    True/False

30. I regularly receive excellent service whenever I shop, travel or
    dine out   True/False

31. I am a creative, original and entertaining presenter   True/False

32. I am fascinated by the human brain and how it work
    True/False

33. I believe I am worth more than I earn   True/False

34. Other people tend to remember what I say   True/False

35. I am physically fit   True/False

36. I am mentally fit   True/False

37. I don't put much emphasis on communicating with animals
    True/False

38. I find ceremonies and rituals boring   True/False

39. Leaders must know how to be followers   True/False

40. I am good at leading some kinds of teams but not others
    True/False

41. There are certain kinds of people I find unutterably boring or a
    waste of time. I try to avoid them · True/False

42. People come to me for help and advice. I happily give it
    True/False

43. In social gatherings I help people to relax, be entertained and
    have fun   True/False

44. Success is largely due to luck   True/False

45. I have a clear goal and vision for my life   True/False

Answers on page 148.

Scoring

1 – 11 Consider your Social Intelligence to be like a giant gold mine that
you have just discovered. If you carry on exploring, wonderful rewards
await you!

12 – 22 This score shows that you have already acquired some of the
basic skills and understandings on the road to Social Intelligence. Try

to use your new knowledge to strengthen your existing skills and develop those areas in which your skills are weaker.

23 – 33 This score indicates that your Social Intelligence skills are above average already. By applying the principles contained in *The Power of Social Intelligence* you will leap into the Brain Star category!

34 – 45 You are a relatively rare person who is reaping the benefits of the development of your Social Intelligence. Following the adage that 'the more you know, the more easy it is to know more', use what you have learned from *The Power of Social Intelligence* to improve dramatically the well-developed skills you already have. As you will have realized, the scope for improvement is infinite.

chapter ten

Social Intelligence is just one of 10 intelligences that we each have. Intelligence has traditionally been divided into three different aspects – Verbal, Numerical and Spatial Intelligences – which are the basis of the standard IQ test. However, we also have Creative, Sensual, Physical, Personal, Sexual and Spiritual Intelligences.

The wonderful thing about our Multiple Intelligences is that they each work with and strengthen all the others in synergy. When you develop one of your intelligences, you simultaneously develop them all.

In this chapter we are going to investigate the application of five of your other Multiple Intelligences to the development of your Social Intelligence. This short chapter is a Workout in itself.

spatial intelligence

Your Spatial Intelligence is the ability of your eye/body system to perceive and successfully negotiate the three-dimensional environment and world around you. It therefore involves your ability to see the relationship of forms and shapes to each other, and to be aware of the space between things. Map reading falls into the domain of this intelligence, as do aspects of body language.

Remember the story of the two businessmen, one from New York and the other from Texas (page 24), who were poles apart when it came to perceptions of personal space? Being aware of the 'comfort zone' for different people is a very important part of Social Intelligence. Use your Spatial Intelligence to become more sensitive in this matter.

Spatial Intelligence also incorporates the ability to place things in the environment such that they make other people feel pleased and comfortable. The ancient Chinese art of Feng Shui is Spatial Intelligence applied to Social Intelligence!

When you are able to influence the environment in which people meet, make sure you give your Spatial Intelligence a long leash ...

physical intelligence

Physical Intelligence involves your ability to be physically co-ordinated, balanced and poised. It also incorporates your eating a healthy diet, and being physically strong, flexible and aerobically fit.

When you develop your Physical Intelligence, you will automatically attract to yourself a wider circle of friends, for people instinctively gravitate towards someone who is healthy, balanced and vibrant.

For a simple indication of this, look at advertisements for anything, and notice that the models the advertisers and marketers use to attract you fit the above description perfectly.

Physical Intelligence also involves your actually making contact with others. As you already know, this is not only pleasurable; it makes both parties more physically healthy by triggering bodily reactions that strengthen the immune system.

Evidence from Japan now also suggests that it will help with your memory as well, as the following study indicates.

Case Study – Want a Better Memory? Make Contact!

A rising number of Japanese are suffering from a form of extreme forgetfulness that is ruining their studies as well as their work performance.

'We are talking about people who can't even remember how to use the copying machine, and who need help to write down step-by-step instructions,' said brain specialist Takashi Tsukiyama.

The complaints of the forgetters include a failure to remember the name of the train station at which they were to alight, the appointments they have made, and even routine functions such as their daily work duties.

Doctor Tsukiyama said that the rate of such cases is on the rise.

The major cause, according to the *Straits Times*, is 'the lack of social interaction among the younger generations in Japan'.

Researchers confirm this, putting the blame on people's increasing social isolation because of their over-reliance on machines, which gradually erode their memory power. Because people nowadays are brought up on video games, the Internet and email communication, they often remain holed up in their homes and have little chance to socialize with others.

Socialization requires a constantly alert and tested memory, with all the senses, the main pillars of memory, in full use and activation.

Researchers conclude that self-isolating computer games and screens retard the memory during childhood, inhibit the development of social skills, and increase the probability that the decline in these two vital areas will continue into adulthood.

Doctor Tsukiyama recommended that people should give themselves a good dose of social interaction at least once a day. He also recommended regular Social Intelligence workouts, in order to keep the brain and body alert and fit, the memory functioning well and the individual's general health maintained.

The news on modern electronic tools such as the Internet is not all bad. If this technology is used to supplement and enhance Social Intelligence, the results can be extremely positive, as the next case study demonstrates.

Case Study – 'Nerds' *Can* Be Good In Herds!

Andrew Oswald, of Warwick University, published at the end of 2001 a survey of 2,500 randomly selected Britons.

Oswald's survey found that net surfers were far more likely to belong to a community group or a voluntary organization than non-surfers. They are also more likely to be regular churchgoers, and to be both better educated and better paid than non-surfers.

Contrary to popular opinion in England, it appears that surfers there have begun to work out a proper balance in their lives between the electronic and the social. They do not, as had been assumed, spend all their days slouching over a computer. They simply watch far less television than the average person.

This suggests that rather than using their free time in passive mode, they actively engage with the Internet and use it to meet other people on a social basis.

These two studies suggest that, as with all new inventions, the Internet can have both negative and positive impacts. If used appropriately, it can add riches to your social life.

sensual intelligence

Sensual Intelligence, the intelligence considered particularly important by Leonardo da Vinci, involves the development and use of your five senses of sight, hearing, smell, taste and touch. Do a mini Mind Map® for each of these five senses, noting on that Mind Map® all the ways in which you can use each of your five senses to enhance your Social Intelligence.

verbal intelligence

Your Verbal Intelligence involves your ability to juggle with the alphabet of letters and the millions of words they make available to you.

This intelligence is measured by the size of your vocabulary, the speed of your ability to make connections between words, the clarity of your expression, the depth of your ability to see logical relationships between words, and the richness of the imagery you use.

As you might imagine, Verbal Intelligence is one of the intelligences most closely connected to Social Intelligence. In normal conversation, your Verbal Intelligence, combined with your body-language, make up the whole package.

In all written communication your Verbal Intelligence is the *whole* package!

Think about how conversations, lectures, speeches, letters, newspapers, magazines, books, the Internet, and poetry have affected *your* life and your relationships with others.

Ensure that you make your body-talk and mouth-talk congruent. Combine what you have learnt in this book with your verbal power to make you a more forceful and interesting speaker, and explore continuingly other possible synergies between the two intelligences.

creative intelligence

As you read the following definition of Creative Intelligence, begin to think about ways in which it can positively boost your Social Intelligence.

Creative Intelligence is your ability to use the full range of your left/right brain skills to come up with original ideas. It incorporates the speed with which you can generate new ideas, your ability to generate ideas that are unusual and unique, your ability to see any situation from a wide range of different perspectives, your ability to take any idea and expand on it, and your ability to use the Brain Principle of Association throughout the entire Creative Thinking process.

Just think what an astonishingly powerful Social Intelligence skill this master intelligence is! Try doing a mini Mind Map® on the ways in which your infinite creative powers can be applied to making the lives of others more colourful, creative, humorous and enjoyable.

social brain boosters

- I am using all the left/right brain skills of my Creative Intelligence to develop my Social Intelligence.
- I am using my body and brain's Physical Intelligence to develop my Social Intelligence.
- I am using my Spatial Intelligence and body-language skills to develop my Social Intelligence.
- I am using my Sensual Intelligence to develop my Social Intelligence.
- I am using the communication skills of my Verbal Intelligence to develop my Social Intelligence.

The last, last word

congratulations!

Congratulations! You have just become a graduate of *The Power of Social Intelligence*. You are now armed to go out into the world (and it *is* a Social world) with a full knowledge of what this vastly important intelligence is and means.

- You are fully aware of the incredible power of your body language and how to use it, and know also how to be an active listener and therefore a great conversationalist. With these skills 'under your belt' you will be able to make the connections you want to, and will naturally begin to shine in social situations.

- Add to this your new and increasingly positive attitude and you will find you are already beginning to do better in negotiations and to make friends in the way you have dreamed.

- Your new social graces and the continued boosting of your Social Intelligence with your other master intelligences mean that you are well on the way to becoming a Social Intelligence Star!

Floreant Dendritae (May your brain cells flourish!)
Tony Buzan

social intelligence survey
questionnaire – answers

1.	True	24.	False
2.	False	25.	True
3.	False	26.	True
4.	True	27.	True
5.	True	28.	True
6.	False	29.	False
7.	False	30.	True
8.	False	31.	True
9.	False	32.	True
10.	False	33.	True
11.	True	34.	True
12.	True	35.	True
13.	False	36.	True
14.	False	37.	False
15.	True	38.	False
16.	True	39.	True
17.	True	40.	False
18.	False	41.	False
19.	False	42.	True
20.	False	43.	True
21.	False	44.	False
22.	True	45.	True
23.	True		

buzan centres
learning & thinking for the 21st century

make the most of your mind
with customised solutions to enhance personal and preofessional performance and increase your Intellectual Capital

- in-company training
- licensing for companies and independent trainers
- 'open' business and public seminars
- educational seminars

We are the ONLY organization thay can license use of the Mind Maps® and associated trademarks

for full details of buzan learning seminars
and information on our range of BrainFriendly® products, including:

- books
- software
- audio and videa tapes
- support materials

send for our brochure

Contact:
Email: Buzan@BuzanCentres.com

Website: www.BuzanCentres.com

Or:

Buzan Centres Ltd (rest of world)
54 Parkstone Road
Poole, Dorset BH15 2PG
Tel: +44 (0) 1202 674676
Fax: +44 (0) 1202 674776

Buzan Centres Inc. (Americas)
PO Box 4, Palm Beach
Florida 33480, USA
Tel (Free Toll in USA): +1 866 896 1024
Tel: +1 734 207 5287

The Brain Trust Charity, #1001012 – invites your contribution to assist brain research into effective processes for the enhancement of learning, thinking and the potential of all.

make the most of your mind ... today!

Other books by Tony Buzan published by Thorsons:

Head First: 10 Ways to Tap into Your Natural Genius
ISBN 0 7225 4046 9

Head Strong: How to get Physically and Mentally Fit
ISBN 0 00 711397 8

The Power of Creative Intelligence
ISBN 0 7225 4050 7

The Power of Spiritual Intelligence
ISBN 0 7225 4047 7

The Power of Verbal Intelligence
ISBN 0 7225 4049 3

Available from all good bookshops, or to order direct from
HarperCollins*Publishers* telephone:

0870 900 250
or
+44 (0)141 306 3296